Code
of
Professional
Ethics
of the
American Institute for
Property and
Liability Underwriters, Inc.

Code
of
Professional
Ethics

of the
American Institute for
Property and
Liability Underwriters, Inc.

Guidelines for Professional Conduct
Disciplinary Rules, Procedures, and Penalties
Advisory Opinions of the Board of Ethical Inquiry

Second Edition • 1991

AMERICAN INSTITUTE FOR
PROPERTY AND LIABILITY UNDERWRITERS
720 Providence Road, Malvern, Pennsylvania 19355-0770

Second Edition • June 1991

Library of Congress Catalog Number 90-083980
International Standard Book Number 0-89463-057-1

Printed in the United States of America

Foreword

This book contains materials that serve a double purpose. First, they codify the ethical standards that both holders of, and candidates for, the Chartered Property Casualty Underwriter designation are expected to maintain. The *Code of Professional Ethics* with its *Canons* and *Rules of Professional Conduct* describes these standards; the *Guidelines* and *Opinions* assist in interpreting them; the *Disciplinary Rules, Procedures, and Penalties* describe the manner in which alleged violations are to be investigated and adjudicated in compliance with the requirements of due process of law.

A second, equally important function of this volume is to serve as a textbook for the Professional Ethics segment of the CPCU curriculum. In this capacity, it is designed to help the CPCU candidate achieve educational objectives that have been formulated in the firm belief that intellectual as well as moral effort is needed in order to create and maintain ethical conduct. Candidates are required to study these materials and are to be tested on their understanding of the subject to the same demanding extent as in the other segments of the CPCU Program.

Each of the materials has been examined in detail and approved by the Board of Ethical Inquiry of the American Institute, as required by the Institute's bylaws, and on whose behalf I wish to express our appreciation to Dr. Ronald C. Horn, CPCU, CLU, Ben H. Williams Professor of Insurance Studies, Hankamer School of Business, Baylor University, who, as author and editor, has contributed far more than any other person to the creation of this text. In addition to his scholarship, his perseverance and his single-mindedness in seeing the "ethics project" through—in a much shorter period of time than anyone thought was possible—has earned him our sincere admiration and gratitude.

James J. Markham, J.D., CPCU, AIC, AIAF
Ethics Counsel
Chairman, Board of Ethical Inquiry
American Institute for Property and Liability
Underwriters

Table of Contents

CODE OF PROFESSIONAL ETHICS
of the
AMERICAN INSTITUTE
FOR PROPERTY AND LIABILITY
UNDERWRITERS, INC.

PREAMBLE

In accordance with the basic purposes for which it was formed, the American Institute for Property and Liability Underwriters is charged with the responsibility of directing a unified effort toward professionalism on the part of CPCUs and CPCU candidates. The American Institute alone is authorized to recognize properly qualified persons with the professional designation, Chartered Property Casualty Underwriter (CPCU), which is conferred only upon individuals who have successfully completed a series of uniform national examinations and have met the experience and ethics requirements established by the Board of Trustees. All holders of the CPCU designation (CPCUs), as well as all CPCU candidates, are expected to comply with both the letter and spirit of the ethical standards set forth explicitly in this *Code of Professional Ethics.*

The basic objective of the *Code* is to serve the public interest, not only by specifying and enforcing the minimum ethical conduct rightfully expected of CPCUs, as professionals, but also by facilitating voluntary compliance with standards considerably higher than the required minimums. Accordingly, the *Code* consists of two kinds of standards, *Canons* and *Rules of Professional Conduct.*

The *Canons* are general standards of an aspirational and inspirational nature, lofty goals reflecting the fundamental spirit of altruism

1

which all true professionals share. They are maxims which on their merits serve as model standards of exemplary professional conduct. The *Canons* also express the general concepts and principles from which the more specific *Rules* are derived.

Unlike the *Canons*, the *Rules* are specific standards of a mandatory and enforceable nature. The *Rules* prescribe the absolute minimum level of ethical conduct required of every CPCU, regardless of occupational position. Any individual subject to the *Code* who violates a *Rule* will be exposed to the possibility of disciplinary action.

In addition to the *Code* per se, the Institute periodically publishes *Guidelines*, advisory *Opinions, Summaries of Previous Rulings*, and similar materials designed to assist CPCUs and CPCU candidates in interpreting the various *Code* provisions, understanding their rationale, and applying them to frequently encountered situations which require ethical judgments.[1] Individuals subject to the *Code* will be exposed to the possibility of disciplinary action for violations of any *Guidelines* which have been incorporated by reference into the *Rules*.[2] In the absence of a *Rule* violation, violations of *Canons* and/or *Guidelines* will not constitute sufficient grounds for disciplinary action. However, it should be acknowledged that in applying the *Rules* and interpreting them uniformly, there may be reference to the general principles and concepts embodied in the *Canons* and to applicable published rulings in previous cases. It also should be stressed that since the use of the CPCU designation is a privilege granted by the Board of Trustees and conditioned upon full compliance with the *Rules of Professional Conduct*, the Board of Trustees reserves the power to suspend or revoke the privilege or approve other penalties recommended by the Board of Ethical Inquiry, which is charged with the responsibility of investigating and adjudicating alleged *Rule* violations. Disciplinary penalties will be imposed as warranted by the severity of the offense and its attendant circumstances. All disciplinary actions will be undertaken in accordance with published procedures and penalties designed to ensure the proper enforcement of the *Rules* within the framework of due process and equal protection of the laws.

---

1. In all Institute ethics publications, the *Rules* and *Guidelines* are grouped and numbered schematically under one *Canon* with which they are closely associated. This format is largely an expositional convenience and should not be allowed to obscure the important *interrelationships* between and among the various *Code* standards which have been approved by the Board of Trustees.

2. For example, the *Guidelines* on uses of the CPCU designation and CPCU key were incorporated by reference in the *Rule R8.1* as of the effective date of this *Code*. Additional *Guidelines* may be incorporated by reference only through approval of additional *Rules* by the Board of Trustees.

After the effective date of this *Code*, all CPCU candidates become subject to the binding effect of the *Rules* when they matriculate with the American Institute and thereafter for as long as they remain candidates. Any such candidate who violates a *Rule* may have conferment of the designation deferred, at the discretion of a duly authorized tribunal, until the tribunal receives convincing proof of the candidate's full and complete rehabilitation.

The *Rules* are also enforceable and binding upon every CPCU whose designation is conferred after the effective date of this *Code*. Any such CPCU who violates a *Rule* may be disciplined by any penalty available to, and imposed by, the enforcing tribunal and/or the Board of Trustees. For a CPCU whose designation was conferred prior to the effective date of this *Code*, no disciplinary penalty will be imposed unless the CPCU voluntarily elects in writing to be bound unconditionally by the mandates of the *Rules*. Nonetheless, all CPCUs who received their designations before the *Code's* effective date are strongly urged to file such a written election with the American Institute, as an act of good faith and in the public interest, in order that all objectives of the *Code* may be achieved. The ultimate regulator of human behavior, of course, emerges from the depths of each individual's conscience as a personal commitment to the highest ethical standards, quite apart from whether those standards may be legally enforced. But when individuals hold themselves out to the public as professionals with common professional standards, the public has a right to expect the observance and reasonable enforcement of those standards.

When there is a good reason for a person subject to this *Code* to be uncertain as to the ethical propriety of a specific activity or type of conduct, that person should refrain from engaging in such activity or conduct until the matter has been clarified. Any CPCU or CPCU candidate who needs assistance in interpreting the *Code* may request an advisory opinion from the American Institute's Board of Ethical Inquiry.[3] Unpublished opinions issued by the Board of Ethical Inquiry are informal and intended solely for the guidance of the individuals to whom they are issued, whereas published *Opinions* are formal and intended for the guidance of all persons subject to the *Code*. Every published *Opinion* except those identified with the prefix "HCS," below, will have a specified effective date, after which it may be used in

---

3. An advisory opinion may be obtained by writing to the Board of Ethical Inquiry, American Institute, 720 Providence Road, Malvern, PA 19355-0770. Only the Board of Ethical Inquiry is authorized to issue such opinions on behalf of the American Institute. In no event will the identity of any inquirer be revealed outside this Board; however, the general nature of an inquiry may be published, together with an advisory *Opinion*, if it warrants a formal, published response.

interpreting and applying the *Rules*.[4] An advisory opinion which pertains exclusively to the application or interpretation of a *Canon* or a *Guideline* will not become binding on any individual unless and until it has been officially approved and has become effective as an addition or amendment to the *Rules of Professional Conduct*. Nevertheless, inquiries concerning *all* aspects of the *Code* are strongly encouraged since the ultimate goal is to *prevent* unethical conduct before it occurs, apart from whether it may result in the imposition of a penalty on a violator. Such inquiries will also stimulate continuing improvements in the *Code* by testing its inherent clarity, depth, and scope.

---

4. *Opinions* with the prefix "HCS" pertain to hypothetical case studies designed for educational purposes and are intended to indicate to the reader the manner in which the Board of Ethical Inquiry might generally react to a broad inquiry on the topic addressed. Because the cases are purely hypothetical, they shall not serve as precedent for any action by the Board of Ethical Inquiry or Ethics Policy Committee. Furthermore, to further enhance their educational value, these opinions frequently contain additional commentary that may not be essential to reach the conclusion.

CANON 1

CPCUs Should Endeavor at All Times to Place the Public Interest Above Their Own.

Rules of Professional Conduct

R1.1   **A CPCU has a duty to understand and abide by all *Rules* of conduct which are prescribed in the Code of Professional Ethics of the American Institute.**

R1.2   **A CPCU shall not advocate, sanction, participate in, cause to be accomplished, otherwise carry out through another, or condone any act which the CPCU is prohibited from performing by the *Rules* of this *Code*.**

Guidelines for Professional Conduct

G1.1   By stipulating at the outset that "CPCUs Should Endeavor at All Times to Place the Public Interest Above Their Own," *Canon 1* serves as the fundamental goal of the entire *Code of Professional Ethics*. The other *Code* Standards are essentially attempts to define the "public interest" (and hence the ethical obligations of CPCUs) in more specific terms. Accordingly, the format of the *Code* is best understood by reading *Canon 1*, asking the question, "how?" and then reading the first two *Rules*. That is to say, how do CPCUs go about endeavoring at all times to place the public interest above their own? Answer: at a *minimum*, by understanding and obeying all the *Rules* in the *Code* (as specified in *R1.1* and *R1.2*) and then, beyond the expected minimums, by *striving* to meet the more lofty standards expressed in the *Canons* and the *Guidelines*.

The aspirational goal of *Canon 1* is more easily expressed than achieved. Indeed, one doubts whether any profession can ultimately make good the claim that all of its practitioners are forever guided by an attitude of altruism and a spirit of unselfish devotion to the needs of others. Nonetheless, a formal commitment to altruism is probably the single most important characteristic which distinguishes professional from unprofessional behavior.

G1.2 In the performance of his or her professional services, a CPCU should avoid even the appearance of impropriety, and should generally do or act each day in a manner that will best serve the CPCU's own professional interests in the long run. This *Guideline*, when taken along with the other provisions of the *Code*, should pose no insurmountable problems of priority in the context of most everyday situations, since the best long-term professional interests of a CPCU ordinarily do not conflict either with the public interest or with other specific interests. However, it should be acknowledged that potential conflicts of interest may arise, or may appear to arise, because many CPCUs simultaneously serve two or more "masters," and they must somehow balance the various interests with their own personal interests and the best interests of the general public. For example, a CPCU who is employed by an insurance company may serve his or her immediate superior, the corporation, the stockholders, the policyholders, agents, and industry associations. An agent may serve his clients, two or more insurers, and his business partners, stockholders, or associates.

Strict compliance with all the *Rules* of this *Code*, including *R1.2*, should enable a CPCU to resolve such potential conflicts of interest which may arise. However, when there is good reason for a person subject to the *Code* to be uncertain as to the ethical propriety of a specific activity or type of conduct, that person should refrain from engaging in such activity or conduct until the matter has been clarified. Any CPCU or CPCU candidate who needs assistance in interpreting the *Code* is encouraged to request an advisory opinion from the American Institute's Board of Ethical Inquiry.

G1.3 The ethical obligation to place the public interest above personal interests or financial gain extends to every CPCU, regardless of whether or not the CPCU's occupational position requires direct contact with actual or prospective insurance consumers.

G1.4 Nothing in these *Guidelines* should be interpreted to mean that insurance purchasers should be given priority over deserving insurance claimants since the needs and best interests of insurance purchasers are in fact served only when all deserving insurance claimants, including third-party liability claimants, are accorded prompt, equitable, and otherwise fair treatment.

CANON 2

CPCUs Should Seek Continually to Maintain and Improve Their Professional Knowledge, Skills, and Competence.

Rules of Professional Conduct

R2.1 **A CPCU shall keep informed on those technical matters that are essential to the maintenance of the CPCU's professional competence in insurance, risk management, or related fields.**

Guidelines for Professional Conduct

G2.1 Though knowledge and skills alone do not ensure that an individual will adhere to high ethical standards, knowledge and skills are requisites to the high levels of competence and performance rightfully expected of all professionals. Indeed, to the extent that an individual purports to be a professional and yet does not maintain high levels of competence and performance, that individual engages in unethical conduct which is in the nature of a misrepresentation.

In order to earn the CPCU designation, every CPCU candidate demonstrated a mastery of insurance and related subjects by successfully completing a series of rigorous qualifying examinations of the American Institute for Property and Liability Underwriters, Inc. However, for any individual to maintain and improve the knowledge and skills which are requisites to high levels of competence and performance, it is essential for that individual to continue studying throughout his or her working life. This is especially true for practitioners in a business like insurance, which is characterized not only by its existing complexities but also by rapid changes in the business and in the legal, economic, and social environment within which it operates.

8

In recognition of the foregoing, each and every CPCU has an *ethical* obligation to engage actively and continuously in appropriate educational activities.

G2.2 At a *minimum*, as specified in *Rule R2.1*, "A CPCU shall keep informed on those technical matters that are essential to the maintenance of the CPCU's professional competence in insurance, risk management, or related fields." Since CPCUs serve as agents, brokers, underwriters, claims representatives, actuaries, risk managers, regulators, company executives and specialists in a wide variety of insurance-related fields, the *Rule* does not attempt to prescribe the specific technical matters that are essential to the maintenance of professional competence in each of the numerous specialties. Instead, it is left to the judgment of each CPCU to decide, in the light of his or her occupational position, the content and form of continuing education that will satisfy the ethical obligation under *R2.1*.

G2.3 A number of other professions have established mandatory continuing education requirements, under the terms of which a member usually faces severe penalties unless he or she periodically certifies that at least one of the specified continuing education options has been met. At present and for the foreseeable future, the Trustees of the American Institute have no plans to require CPCUs to certify periodically that they have met the obligations under *Rule R2.1*. However, because the maintenance of professional competence is considered a minimum obligation of every CPCU, it has been given the status of a *Rule* under the *Code*. The Board of Ethical Inquiry will investigate alleged violations of *Rule 2.1*, and it may impose upon violators such penalties as are warranted. Furthermore, if a CPCU is accused of violating any other *Rule* in the *Code*, the Board may, at its discretion, require the accused to furnish evidence of compliance with *Rule 2.1*.

G2.4 Beyond the minimum continuing education requirements referred to in *Rule 2.1*, all CPCUs are urged to engage in such additional pursuits as will meet the aspirational goal, under *Canon 2*, of *improving* their professional knowledge, skills, and competence.

For example, the Board of Ethical Inquiry suggests that every CPCU should, within each three-year interval commencing with the conferment date of his or her designation and ending with the date of his or her retirement from the insurance profession, actively participate in and complete *at least one* of the following activities:

a. Participate as an attendee, a discussion leader, lecturer, moderator, or panelist in educational forums, seminars, or courses pertaining to risk, insurance, or related subjects in some combination which will amount to a total of at least forty hours of active educational involvement;

   OR

b. Serve as an instructor or a discussion leader of at least one full course involving insurance and/or related subjects and amounting to no less than twenty-five hours of classroom instruction;

   OR

c. Successfully complete at least one college or university course of no less than three hours' credit, or obtain continuing education units (CEUs) equivalent to three hours of college or university credit in a subject which will maintain or enhance the CPCU's professional competence;

   OR

d. Pass an examination in the series leading to the CLU, FSA, FCAS, CPA, CFA, or FLMI professional designation;

   OR

e. Retake and pass a CPCU examination (a reduced examination fee will be available to any person who already holds the CPCU designation);

   OR

f. Pass an examination leading to an Insurance Institute of America designation such as the Accredited Advisor in Insurance, the Associate in Risk Management, Claims, Underwriting, Management, Loss Control Management, Premium Auditing, Research and Planning, Insurance Accounting and Finance, Marine Insurance Management, Automation Management, Reinsurance, or similar designation awarded by the Institute;

   OR

g. Author or coauthor (1) a published book or mongraph on insurance or a closely related subject, (2) an article on insurance or a closely related subject and have it accepted for publication in the *CPCU Journal* or another recognized professional journal, or (3) study materials used in an educational course of the type listed in option b. above;

   OR

h. Engage in a regular program of independent study, preferably a program which has been approved by the American

Institute's Board of Ethical Inquiry;

OR

i. Engage in an appropriate combination of the foregoing educational activities.

CANON 3

CPCUs Should Obey All Laws and Regulations, and Should Avoid Any Conduct or Activity Which Would Cause Unjust Harm to Others.

Rules of Professional Conduct

R3.1   **In the conduct of business or professional activities, a CPCU shall not engage in any act or omission of a dishonest, deceitful, or fraudulent nature.**

R3.2   **A CPCU shall not allow the pursuit of financial gain or other personal benefit to interfere with the exercise of sound professional judgment and skills.**

R3.3   **A CPCU will be subject to disciplinary action for the violation of any law or regulation, to the extent that such violation suggests the likelihood of professional misconduct in the future.**

Guidelines for Professional Conduct

G3.1   A CPCU should neither misrepresent nor conceal a fact or information which is material to determining the suitability, efficacy, scope, or limitations of an insurance contract or surety bond. Nor should a CPCU materially misrepresent or conceal the financial condition, or the quality of services, of any insurer or reinsurer. The extent to which a CPCU should volunteer information and facts must necessarily be left to sound professional judgment of what is required under the circumstances. This *Guideline* is intended to illustrate the kinds of acts and omissions which can be "dishonest, deceitful, or fraudulent," in violation of *Rule R3.1*, and which normally "would cause unjust harm to others," thus violating the spirit of *Canon 3*.

G3.2   A CPCU should not, to the detriment of the insuring public, engage in any business practice or activity designed to restrict fair competition. However, this *Guideline* does not prohibit a CPCU's participation in a legally enforceable covenant not to compete, in a rating bureau, or in a similar activity specifically sanctioned or required by law.

G3.3   In the performance of the CPCU's own occupational function, a CPCU should not deliberately achieve or seek to achieve, at the expense of the uninformed, financial gains for the CPCU, or the CPCU's employer, which are unconscionable relative to the customary gains for the quantity and quality of services actually rendered.

Generally, no CPCU should seek or accept compensation which is neither for nor commensurate with professional services actually rendered or to be rendered. Nor should any CPCU seek or accept compensation under any other terms, conditions, or circumstances which would violate any *Canon*, *Guideline*, or *Rule* in this *Code*. However, nothing in this *Guideline* is intended to prohibit the seeking or acceptance of gifts from family or personal friends, income from investments, or income from any other activity which would neither (a) prevent or inherently impair the free and complete exercise of the CPCU's sound professional judgment and skills nor (b) otherwise violate this *Code*.

A CPCU should not perform professional services under terms, conditions, or circumstances which would prevent or inherently impair the free and complete exercise of the CPCU's sound professional judgment and skills. This guideline does not prohibit a CPCU from being compensated under the terms of a legally acceptable commission arrangement since such an arrangement, in itself, does not prevent or inherently impair the CPCU's sound professional judgment and skills. But it does serve to remind a CPCU so compensated of his or her ethical obligation to avoid any recommendation to a consumer of the CPCU's services that would increase the CPCU's compensation, unless such recommendation clearly meets the consumer's legitimate needs and best interests. The guideline also serves to remind every CPCU, regardless of his or her basis of compensation, of the ethical obligation to render fully such services as are contemplated and rightfully owed under the terms of the applicable compensation arrangement.

G3.4   While the Institute's standards of ethical conduct are by no means limited to the duties and obligations imposed upon

CPCUs by the laws and regulations which govern the conduct of all insurance practitioners, obedience to and respect for law and regulatory authority should be viewed as an absolute minimum standard of professional conduct below which no CPCU should fall. The potential consequences of violating this admonition extend beyond those which may fall upon the violator since one CPCU may indeed bring discredit upon the CPCU designation, and thus all who hold it, by violating laws or regulations which govern the conduct of a CPCU's business activities.

A CPCU is obligated to keep fully informed of each and every law and regulation governing or otherwise pertaining to his business activities. In so doing, a CPCU should not hesitate to seek interpretive assistance from the appropriate regulatory officials and/or retain the services of competent legal counsel. When in doubt as to the legality of a particular kind of business conduct or activity, the CPCU should refrain from such conduct or activity.

A CPCU may not plead lack of knowledge as a defense for improper conduct under *Rule 3.3* unless the CPCU can demonstrate that he or she had made a reasonable effort in good faith to obtain such knowledge, and it was not available.

The American Institute does *not* condone violations of *any* of the laws and regulations governing citizens in a civilized society. Indeed, *Canon 3* reminds CPCUs that they "should obey all laws and regulations." In establishing the objectives for the Institute's *Code of Professional Ethics*, however, the Trustees decided to confine the enforceable *Rules* to matters of business or professional conduct since it was felt that enforcing standards of personal conduct and morality lie outside the Institute's proper role. But drawing an appropriate dividing line between business and personal conduct is no easy task. Should a CPCU have his or her designation taken away, or be otherwise disciplined by the Institute, for getting a parking ticket? A speeding ticket? For violating the drug laws? For alcoholism, child abuse, rape? For misdemeanors, felonies, or murder? However regrettable such crimes and law violations may be, should they subject the guilty individual to additional disciplinary action by the Institute?

After over two years of study and upon the advice of legal counsel, the Institute Trustees approved *Rule R3.3*. It stipulates that a CPCU "will be subject to disciplinary action for the violation of *any* law or regulation. . .*to the extent that* such violation suggests the likelihood of professional misconduct in the future" (emphasis supplied). It does not say a CPCU *will be* disciplined for violating any law or regulation. It says a CPCU will be *subject to* disciplinary action. . .to the extent that (a violation) suggests the likelihood of professional misconduct in the future. The *Rule* thus leaves it up to the Board of Ethical Inquiry to decide (a) whether any disciplinary action should be taken and (b) what penalty, if any, should be imposed, but it also specifies the criterion that will be used by the Board in making such judgments. The test will be whether the Board feels a particular violation is sufficient evidence that *professional* misconduct is *likely* in the future.

With respect to an actual or alleged violation of any *Rule* in the *Code*, the published Disciplinary Rules and Procedures of the Institute permit the CPCU or CPCU candidate an opportunity to provide convincing proof of full and complete rehabilitation, in which case the action will be dismissed or the previously imposed penalty revoked (see the *Disciplinary Rules* for details).

CANON 4

CPCUs Should Be Diligent in the Performance of Their Occupational Duties and Should Continually Strive to Improve the Functioning of the Insurance Mechanism.

Rules of Professional Conduct

R4.1 **A CPCU shall competently and consistently discharge his or her occupational duties.**

R4.2 **A CPCU shall support efforts to effect such improvements in claims settlement, contract design, investment, marketing, pricing, reinsurance, safety engineering, underwriting, and other insurance operations as will both inure to the benefit of the public and improve the overall efficiency with which the insurance mechanism functions.**

Guidelines for Professional Conduct

G4.1 From one who purports to be a true professional, the public has a right to expect both competence, in the sense of abilities, and diligent performance, in the sense of consistently applying those abilities in the service of others. Thus, to complement *Rule R2.1*, which obligates a CPCU to maintain professional competence by keeping informed, the Institute also promulgated *Rule R4.1*, which stipulates that "a CPCU shall competently and consistently *discharge* his or her occupational duties."

Although the Board of Ethical Inquiry earnestly believes that diligent performance should be an ethical obligation of all professionals, including CPCUs, the Board will not intervene or arbitrate between the parties in an employment or contractual relationship or civil dispute. Nor does the Board feel that the Institute's disciplinary procedures should become a substitute for legal and other remedies available to such parties. In the event of an alleged violation of *Rule R4.1*, therefore, the Board will hear the case only after all other remedies have been exhausted, and it generally will take disciplinary action only under circumstances where (1) a proven violation has caused unjust harm to another person, and the violation brings substantial discredit upon the CPCU designation; or (2) it would otherwise be in the *public* interest to take disciplinary action under the ethics code.

G4.2 In addition to competently and consistently discharging his or her own occupational duties, a CPCU is obligated by *Rule R4.2* "to support efforts to effect such improvements (in insurer functions and operations) as will both inure to the benefit of the public and improve the overall efficiency with which the insurance mechanism functions." Note that the obligation is to support the kinds of improvements which will *both* improve the efficiency of the insurance mechanism *and* benefit the public. The drafters of the *Code* worded the rule in this fashion to focus attention on the fact that it is possible to effect improvements in insurer efficiency and profitability at least in the short run, in a manner contrary to the public interest. Granted, it is sometimes very difficult to determine whether a proposed change will both improve overall efficiency and inure to the benefit of the public, but the ethical obligation, consistent with the theme expressed in *Canon 1*, is to support *efforts* to effect such improvements. The kinds of efforts which satisfy both criteria, and which the Board feels a CPCU should support, are illustrated in the *Guidelines* immediately following.

G4.3 A CPCU should assist in improving the language, suitability, adaptability, and general efficacy of insurance contracts and surety bonds.

G4.4 A CPCU should assist in ensuring protection and security for the public, and in maintaining and improving the integrity of the insurance institution, by helping to preserve and improve the financial strength of all private insurers.

G4.5 A CPCU should assist in providing an adequate supply of insurance and surety bonds to meet public demands and needs.

G4.6 A CPCU should do the utmost to assist in minimizing the cost to the public of insurance and suretyship, without compromising the quality of benefits or services they provide, not only by helping to improve the operational efficiency of insurers and their representatives but also by contributing to the solution of economic, legal, political and other social problems which demonstrably increase the cost of insurance and suretyship without enhancing their quality or otherwise improving the public well-being. Examples of such problems include, though are not limited to, inflation, unemployment, crime, inequities and inefficiencies in our legal system, inequities and inefficiencies in our health care delivery system, riots, floods and other highly destructive natural catastrophes, and the physical deterioration of property in the nation's cities. The ready availability of insurance alone will not solve such problems. And a CPCU should not neglect his or her personal duty, as a good citizen and a professional, to become actively involved in the search for underlying causes of, and long-run solutions to, such problems.

G4.7 Because of a CPCU's professional capabilities and firsthand knowledge of a tragic magnitude of human and dollar losses suffered annually, a CPCU should assume an especially active role in private and public loss prevention and reduction efforts. A CPCU should do the utmost to preserve each and every human life, maintain and improve the physical and mental health of all human beings, and prevent the damage, destruction, and abstraction of property.

G4.8 A CPCU should make an effort to participate in and support research which promises to assist in improving the functioning of the private insurance mechanism and/or in reducing losses of life, health, or property.

G4.9 The ethical obligation under this *Code* to strive for improvement in the functioning of the private insurance mechanism does not bar a CPCU from serving in the public sector. Nor does it bar a CPCU, as an *individual* citizen, from supporting a governmental role in providing economic security for the citizenry. But a CPCU should be mindful of the restriction imposed by *Rule R8.4*, and should avoid even the appearance of speaking on behalf of the Institute, especially on political matters.

CANON 5

CPCUs Should Assist in Maintaining and Raising Professional Standards in the Insurance Business.

Rules of Professional Conduct

R5.1 A CPCU shall support personnel policies and practices which will attract qualified individuals to the insurance business, provide them with ample and equal opportunities for advancement, and encourage them to aspire to the highest levels of professional competence and achievement.

R5.2 A CPCU shall encourage and assist qualified individuals who wish to pursue CPCU or other studies which will enhance their professional competence.

R5.3 A CPCU shall support the development, improvement, and enforcement of such laws, regulations, and codes as will foster competence and ethical conduct on the part of all insurance practitioners and inure to the benefit of the public.

R5.4 A CPCU shall not withhold information or assistance officially requested by appropriate regulatory authorities who are investigating or prosecuting any alleged violation of the laws or regulations governing the qualifications or conduct of insurance practitioners.

Guidelines for Professional Conduct

G5.1 A CPCU should assist in the raising of professional standards in the insurance business. At a minimum, every CPCU should conduct his or her own business activities in a manner which will, by the CPCU's precept and example, inspire other practitioners to do likewise.

G5.2 Both the insuring public and the insurance industry will benefit from continued growth in the number of insurance practi-

18

tioners who achieve a high level of professional attainment. Thus, *Rule R5.2* stipulates that "A CPCU shall encourage and assist qualified individuals who wish to pursue CPCU or other studies which will enhance their professional competence."

A CPCU should share with all other insurance practitioners, as well as fellow CPCUs, the benefits of the CPCU's professional attainments. A CPCU's conduct should be guided by a spirit of altruistic concern for the public interest, and the public interest is best served when all insurance practitioners are well informed.

Moreover, any professional who has acquired a unified body of knowledge is invariably indebted to innumerable predecessors and contemporaries for having made available the benefits of their professional attainments, that is, for having shared freely with others their knowledge, accumulated experiences, skills, and insights into understanding. So also should a CPCU, as a professional who has subscribed to high ethical standards, share freely with contemporaries and, thus, future generations, the benefits of his or her own professional attainments, apart from any hope or expectation of immediate financial gain, because of the CPCU's ethical obligations to repay an indebtedness to forebears, contribute to the efficient advancement of human knowledge, and manifest an altruistic concern for the public interest.

A CPCU should support and participate in educational activities which will assist other practitioners in their professional development. Examples of such activities include seminars, lectures, research projects, teaching, preparation of educational materials for training programs, and preparation of professional articles for professional or lay publications. In writing or speaking publicly as a CPCU, however, the CPCU should maintain the dignity and high professional standards appropriate to the designation.

This *Guideline* does not obligate a CPCU to divulge trade secrets or other information which would put the CPCU at a competitive disadvantage. Instead, it serves as a reminder that just as the truly professional physician demonstrates a commitment to the advancement of medicine by sharing his or her knowledge and experiences with other physicians and aspiring physicians, so also should a CPCU play a role in the development of the field of insurance, in part by sharing knowledge with other practitioners as well as students.

CANON 6

CPCUs Should Strive to Establish and Maintain Dignified and Honorable Relationships with Those Whom They Serve, with Fellow Insurance Practitioners, and with Members of Other Professions.

Rules of Professional Conduct

R6.1 **A CPCU shall keep informed on the legal limitations imposed upon the scope of his or her professional activities.**

R6.2 **A CPCU shall not disclose to another person any confidential information entrusted to, or obtained by, the CPCU in the course of the CPCU's business or professional activities, unless a disclosure of such information is required by law or is made to a person who necessarily must have the information in order to discharge legitimate occupational or professional duties.**

R6.3 **In rendering or proposing to render professional services for others, a CPCU shall not knowingly misrepresent or conceal any limitations on the CPCU's ability to provide the quantity or quality of professional services required by the circumstances.**

Guidelines for Professional Conduct

G6.1 First and foremost by exhibiting high levels of professional competence and ethical conduct, a CPCU should constantly strive to *merit* the confidence and respect of those whom they serve, fellow practitioners, and members of other professions.

G6.2 A CPCU should strive to establish and maintain dignified and honorable relationships with competitors, as well as with other fellow practitioners.

G6.3 A CPCU should strive to establish and maintain dignified and honorable relationships with members of other professions, including but not limited to law, medicine, and accounting. The insurance industry relies heavily on the expertise and cooperation of such professionals in fulfilling its obligation to deliver insurance benefits promptly and otherwise render high quality insurance services to the public.

G6.4   Like other professionals, a CPCU should maintain the knowledge and skills necessary to exercise independent judgment in the performance of his or her professional services. However, a CPCU should always be mindful of his or her personal limitations. A CPCU should not hesitate to seek the counsel of other professionals, therefore, not only at the request of those whom the CPCU may serve but also on the CPCU's own initiative, particularly in doubtful or difficult situations or when the quality of professional service may otherwise by enhanced by such consultation.

G6.5   A CPCU is obligated to keep fully informed on any and all legal limitations imposed upon the scope of his or her professional activities. A CPCU should always exercise caution to avoid engaging in, or giving the appearance of engaging in, the unauthorized practice of law. However, nothing herein should be construed as prohibiting the practice of law by a CPCU who is otherwise qualified by virtue of his or her admission to the bar.

G6.6   Beyond the obligations under *Rule R6.2*, a CPCU should exercise caution and sound judgment in dealing with any confidential or privileged information.

CANON 7

CPCUs Should Assist in Improving the Public Understanding of Insurance and Risk Management.

Rules of Professional Conduct

R7.1   **A CPCU shall support efforts to provide members of the public with objective information concerning their risk management and insurance needs, and the products, services, and techniques which are available to meet their needs.**

R7.2   **A CPCU shall not misrepresent the benefits, costs, or limitations of any risk management technique or any product or service of an insurer.**

Guidelines for Professional Conduct

G7.1   Fulfillment of all the public's insurance needs would appreciably enhance the economic and social well-being of society. But the public's insurance needs can be fully met only if every citizen recognizes his or her insurance needs and appreciates the importance of seeking competent and ethical assistance in analyzing and meeting these needs. The achievement of this result requires the combined efforts of all knowledgeable insurance professionals. Accordingly, every CPCU should assist in every practical manner to improve the public understanding of insurance and risk management even if the CPCU does not specialize in insurance education, marketing, claims settlement, safety engineering, advertising, or other professional activities which provide frequent opportunities to communicate directly to the public.

G7.2   A CPCU should keep abreast of legislation, changing conditions and/or other developments which may affect the insuring public, and should assist in keeping the public informed of such.

G7.3 In order to contribute to a better public understanding of insurance and risk management, it is essential for every CPCU to maintain and improve his or her own knowledge and communicative skills. However, no CPCU should hesitate to admit freely that he or she does not know the answer to a question. Nor should a CPCU attempt to answer such a question if it lies outside the realm of the CPCU's professional competence, authority, or proper function.

G7.4 A CPCU should neither engage in nor condone deceptive advertising or business practices which significantly mislead the public or otherwise contribute to the widespread misunderstanding or misuse of insurance. The minimum goal of all a CPCU's communications with the public should be to provide objective and factual information.

G7.5 It is highly desirable for the public to recognize its overall risk management needs and the limitations and advantages of insurance in meeting such needs. For instance, a CPCU should seize every opportunity to stress the importance of loss prevention and reduction in any well-conceived risk management program.

G7.6 *Rule R7.1* stipulates that "A CPCU shall support efforts to provide members of the public with objective information concerning their risk management and insurance needs, and the products, services, and techniques which are available to meet their needs." Both in the *Rules* and in the *Guidelines* above, the needs referred to are those which exist (at a point in time, understood) and the products, services, and techniques referred to are those which are available (at a point in time, understood). Neither the *Rules* nor the *Guidelines* require a CPCU to support lobbying efforts or proposed legislation, or the taking of positions on controversial issues. Nor do any of the *Code* standards prohibit a CPCU from engaging in such activities, in his or her own name and as an individual. However, a CPCU who elects to engage in such activities should take great care to avoid violating *Rule R8.4.*

CANON 8

CPCUs Should Honor the Integrity and Respect the Limitations Placed upon the Use of the CPCU Designation.

Rule of Professional Conduct

R8.1   **A CPCU shall use the CPCU designation and the CPCU key only in accordance with the relevant *Guidelines* promulgated by the American Institute.**

R8.2   **A CPCU shall not attribute to the mere possession of the designation depth or scope of knowledge, skills, and professional capabilities greater than those demonstrated by successful completion of the CPCU program.**

R8.3   **A CPCU shall not make unfair comparisons between a person who holds the CPCU designation and one who does not.**

R8.4   **A CPCU shall not write, speak, or act in such a way as to lead another to reasonably believe the CPCU is officially representing the American Institute, unless the CPCU has been duly authorized to do so by the American Institute**

Guidelines for Professional Conduct

G8.1   *Rule 8.1* of the *Code of Professional Ethics* stipulates that "A CPCU shall use the CPCU designation and the CPCU key only in accordance with the relevant *Guidelines* promulgated by the American Institute." These *Guidelines*, which define and impose restrictions upon the privilege to use the CPCU designation and key, are set forth below. They are designed to prevent undignified commercialization of the designation, unfair comparisons with able and well-established insurance practitioners who do not hold the designation, and other unethical practices which are inconsistent with the professional concepts

24

which CPCU represents. Specifically, every CPCU has an ethical obligation to comply with the following minimum standards:

a. The designation Chartered Property Casualty Underwriter, the initials CPCU, and the CPCU key may be used only in a dignified and professional manner.

   1. The designation or initials may be used after the holder's name on business cards, stationery, office advertising, signed articles, business and professional listings, and telephone listings, except where such use would conflict with the provisions of subparagraph a.3. below.

   2. The CPCU key (actual size or reduced, but not enlarged) may be imprinted only on business cards and stationery used exclusively by CPCUs. Copies of the CPCU key suitable for reproduction are available from the American Institute.

   3. The CPCU designation being personal in nature, the designation itself, the initials CPCU, and the CPCU key are not to be used as part of a firm, partnership, or corporate name, trademark, or logo, or affixed to any object, product, property, or for any purpose whatsoever, except by the American Institute.

b. The designation Chartered Property Casualty Underwriter, the initials CPCU, and the CPCU key may be used to announce the conferment of the designation.

   1. News releases prepared by the American Institute are mailed to all new CPCU designees. Only these approved releases, with the addition of personal biographical information, may be used by individual CPCU designees in preparing material for the business and community press.

   2. Announcement cards may be purchased from the American Institute, or printed locally using a reproduction copy supplied by the Institute without charge, to send to friends, relatives, associates, and clients.

   3. The American Institute encourages employers of new designees to publish in company publications articles congratulating the new designees. The American Institute's official listing of new designees, published at the time of the conferment ceremony, should be used to verify the names of new designees. Copies of the CPCU

key are available from the American Institute for reproduction in such articles.

4. The American Institute encourages the appearance of dignified advertisements congratulating new designees on earning the CPCU designation. Copies of the CPCU key are available from the American Institute for reproduction in such advertisements. These advertisements must be strictly congratulatory in nature, however, and should not include the business conducted by the firm, the lines of insurance carried by the firm, the firm's telephone number, or any copy soliciting business.

c. The designation Chartered Property Casualty Underwriter, the initials CPCU, and the CPCU key may be used by the Society of CPCU in a manner which complies with the *Rules* and *Guidelines* of the American Institute's *Code of Professional Ethics*, and which has first been authorized in writing by the American Institute's Management Council.

d. The designation Chartered Property Casualty Underwriter, the initials CPCU, and the CPCU key may not be used in any manner which violates a *Rule* of the *Code of Professional Ethics*. *Rules 8.2*, *8.3*, and *8.4* deserve special mention in this context since they relate directly to, and impose restrictions upon, the privilege to use the CPCU designation.

e. The designation Chartered Property Casualty Underwriter, the initials CPCU, and the CPCU key may be used in any other manner which has received prior approval in writing from the American Institute's Management Council.

Any questions regarding the interpretation of these *Guidelines* should be directed to the American Institute's Board of Ethical Inquiry. A prompt response will be made to all such requests.

G8.2 *Rule R8.2* stipulates that "A CPCU shall not attribute to the *mere possession of the designation* (emphasis supplied) depth or scope of knowledge, skills, and professional capabilities greater than those demonstrated by successful completion of the CPCU program." Unless this *Rule* is strictly observed by all CPCUs, the public will be misled and the integrity of the designation, as well as the integrity of the violator, will be significantly diminished.

CPCUs can be justifiably proud of having passed the rigorous qualifying exams and of having met the ethical and experience requirements imposed by the American Institute. But the CPCU curriculum, comprehensive though it is, does not in itself make a person an expert in every insurance and insurance-related area. Moreover, the CPCU curriculum has been periodically altered over the years to accommodate revised educational needs and objectives.

Consider, for instance, the case of an agent whose CPCU designation was conferred in a year prior to 1978. Such an agent would clearly violate *R8.2* if he led a prospective client to believe that the possession of his CPCU designation made him a qualified expert in life, health, or group insurance, particularly since the curriculum at that time provided little or no study or testing in these areas. The agent might otherwise have become a qualified expert in life, health, or group insurance, perhaps through experience and/or other formal educational programs, but it would be unethical to attribute this expertise to his possession of the CPCU designation per se. In short, the public is protected and the integrity of the designation and its holder are best preserved by avoiding any misrepresentations of the nature and significance of the CPCU designation.

CANON 9

CPCUs Should Assist in Maintaining the Integrity of the Code of Professional Ethics.

Rules of Professional Conduct

R9.1 A CPCU shall not initiate or support the CPCU candidacy of any individual known by the CPCU to engage in business practices which violate the ethical standards prescribed by this *Code*.

R9.2 A CPCU possessing unprivileged information concerning an alleged violation of this *Code* shall, upon request, reveal such information to the tribunal or other authority empowered by the American Institute to investigate or act upon the alleged violation.

R9.3 A CPCU shall report promptly to the American Institute any information concerning the use of the CPCU designation by an unauthorized person.

Guidelines for Professional Conduct

G9.1 It is *not* an objective of the American Institute to achieve growth in the number of CPCUs at the expense of professional standards, but rather to encourage more qualified individuals to meet the high standards which have always characterized the CPCU designation requirements. A CPCU should assist in upholding the experience, educational, and ethical standards prescribed for prospective CPCU designees by the American Institute for Property and Liability Underwriters, Inc.

G9.2 A CPCU should assist the American Institute in preserving the integrity of the *Code of Professional Ethics*, first and foremost by *voluntarily* complying with both the letter and the spirit of the *Code*. Ultimately, however, the public can be protected and the integrity of the *Code* can be maintained only if the *Code* is strictly but fairly enforced, and this, in turn, can be achieved only if *Code* violations are promptly brought to the attention of the proper officials. Although a CPCU should not become a self-appointed investigator or judge on matters properly left to the Board of Ethical Inquiry, every CPCU should comply with the mandates of *Rules R9.1, R9.2,* and *R9.3.* Except for the comparatively rare but troublesome situation covered by *R9.3,* whether a CPCU should *volunteer* adverse information is left to the judgment of the CPCU.

G9.3   Upon request, a CPCU should serve on such committees, boards, or tribunals as are prescribed by the Institute for the administration or enforcement of the *Code*. A CPCU is obligated to disqualify himself or herself from such service (i) if the CPCU believes, in good conscience, that he or she could not serve in a fair and impartial manner or (ii) upon request.

DISCIPLINARY RULES, PROCEDURES, AND PENALTIES
for the enforcement of the
CODE OF PROFESSIONAL ETHICS
of the
AMERICAN INSTITUTE
FOR PROPERTY AND LIABILITY
UNDERWRITERS, INC.

I. Applicability

A. In accordance with Articles I and IV of the Bylaws of the American Institute, the Board of Trustees has established educational, experience, and ethical standards which must be met by every individual who seeks the privilege of being designated a Chartered Property Casualty Underwriter (CPCU). The ethical standards are set forth explicitly in the *Code of Professional Ethics*.

The *Code* consists of a preamble and two kinds of standards, *Canons* and *Rules of Professional Conduct*. Whereas the *Canons* are general standards of an aspirational and inspirational nature, the *Rules* are specific standards of a mandatory and enforceable nature. The *Rules* prescribe the absolute minimum level of ethical conduct required of every individual subject to the *Code*.

B. Pursuant to the agreements stipulated in the application for admission to CPCU candidacy, all CPCU candidates voluntarily agree to be judged by the ethical standards prescribed by the Board of Trustees. Thus, at the time they matriculate with the American Institute and thereafter for as long as they remain candidates, all CPCU candidates are subject to the binding effect of the *Rules of Professional Conduct*.

C. The *Rules of Professional Conduct* are also enforceable and binding upon all CPCUs whose designations are conferred after 1 July 1976. However, by resolution of the Board of Trustees, the earliest enforcement date shall be deferred for such CPCUs until 1 July 1977.

D. As respects CPCUs whose designations were conferred prior to 1 July 1976, the earliest enforcement date shall be deferred until the first day following the filing, if any, of an individual CPCU's voluntary written election to be bound by the *Rules of Professional Conduct* or, if later, 1 July 1977.

II. Jurisdiction

A. The investigation of an alleged violation of the *Code of Professional Ethics* shall be carried out by a person or persons designated by the Chairman of the Board of Ethical Inquiry.

B. As authorized by the Bylaws, adjudication of alleged violations of the *Rules of Professional Conduct* shall be by the Board of Ethical Inquiry and the Ethics Policy Committee.

III. Ethics Policy Committee, Board of Ethical Inquiry, Ethics Counsel

A. *Ethics Policy Committee of the Board of Trustees.* The Ethics Policy Committee shall consist of the Chairman of the Board of Trustees, "ex officio," and two (2) additional Board of Trustees members elected by the Board of Trustees. The President shall designate one of the elected members as Chairman of this committee. The Ethics Policy Committee shall have responsibility for reviewing matters of policy associated with all Institute ethics activities, making recommendations to the Executive Committee and the Board of Trustees, and providing for liaison with the Society of Chartered Property and Casualty Underwriters on ethical policy considerations. The Ethics Policy Committee shall promulgate the specific disciplinary procedures and penalties to be used in enforcing the *Code of Professional Ethics* of the American Institute and shall have the authority to approve such periodic changes in the disciplinary procedures and penalties as may be necessary or desirable. The Ethics Policy Committee shall also have the authority to act on behalf of the Board of Trustees on all recommendations of the Board of Ethical Inquiry concerning disciplinary matters. All revocations and suspensions of the privilege to use the CPCU designation shall be reported in writing to the Board.

B. *Board of Ethical Inquiry.* The Board of Ethical Inquiry shall consist of eight (8) members appointed by the President of the American Institute subject to the advice and consent of the Ethics Policy Committee. All members shall be CPCUs, and together they shall constitute, as nearly as is practical, a representative cross section of the occupational backgrounds and other pertinent characteristics of all CPCUs. One member shall be the Ethics Counsel, a staff officer of the American Institute other than the President, who shall serve ex officio as nonvoting chairperson. The other seven (7) members shall not be full-time employees of the American Institute or the Society of CPCU.

When the Board of Ethical Inquiry is first selected, two of its voting members shall be appointed for a term of one year, two for a term of two years, and three for a term of three years. All terms thereafter shall be for three years, and no voting member shall serve for more than two full consecutive terms. Except for the members comprising the first Board of Ethical Inquiry, the terms of new members shall commence on the first day of January, and four members shall constitute a quorum.

The Board of Ethical Inquiry shall be responsible for implementing established and approved ethics policy. The principal functions of the Board of Ethical Inquiry shall be to certify that CPCU candidates have met all ethics requirements, issue opinions to CPCUs and CPCU candidates who request assistance in interpreting or applying the *Code of Professional Ethics*, instigate independent investigations of the facts in cases involving alleged *Rule* violations under the *Code*, and serve as the tribunal to hear and decide cases involving alleged *Rule* violations.

The Board of Ethical Inquiry shall when it deems appropriate, (1) promulgate and publish guidelines to supplement the *Code of Professional Ethics*, (2) summarize and publish the rulings of the tribunal in cases brought before it, (3) recommend amendments and additions to the *Code*, improvements in the disciplinary and enforcement procedures, changes in ethics policy, and (4) engage in such other activities which will assist in the implementation of approved ethics policies. The Board of Ethical Inquiry may carry out some of its functions through Institute staff, consultants, investigators, or subcommittees, but all disciplinary actions and published materials must be approved by a majority of its voting members.

The Chairperson of the Board of Ethical Inquiry shall be the Ethics Counsel of the American Institute who shall be the administrative head of the Board, and shall preside at all meetings of the Board, but the chairperson may not participate in the deliberations of the Board in its capacity as a disciplinary tribunal.

C. *Ethics Counsel.* Ethics Counsel, hereinafter referred to as Counsel, in addition to the duties described in III. B. above, shall have the power and duty to

    (1)   investigate all matters involving an alleged violation of the *Code*;

    (2)   dispose of all matters (subject to the provisions of IV. B. and C. below) either by dismissal or the prosecution of

formal charges before a Hearing Panel or the Ethics Policy Committee of the Board of Trustees;

(3) appear at hearings conducted with respect to petitions for reinstatement by CPCUs whose designations have been suspended or revoked; cross-examine witnesses testifying in support of the motion and marshal available evidence, if any, in opposition thereto; and

(4) maintain permanent records of all ethics matters processed and the disposition thereof.

IV. Procedures

A. *Complaints.*

(1) All complaints alleging a violation of the *Code of Professional Ethics* shall be submitted in writing to Counsel and signed by the complainant.

(2) If, after the investigation described in paragraph B. below, it is decided to proceed with formal disciplinary proceedings, a copy of the complaint shall be furnished by Counsel to the person or persons against whom the complaint is lodged.

(3) Counsel, in accordance with procedures specified below, shall determine whether the complaint is of sufficient merit to warrant submission to the Board of Ethical Inquiry.

B. *Procedures Concerning Alleged Violation of the Code by CPCUs.*

(1) *Investigation.* All investigations, whether upon complaint or otherwise, shall be initiated and conducted by Counsel. Upon the conclusion of an investigation, Counsel may dismiss complaints which, in Counsel's opinion, are frivolous, prima facie without merit, or for the lack of jurisdiction. The dismissal of any other complaint by Counsel may be effected only after Counsel has secured the concurrence of two voting members of the Board of Ethical Inquiry. Counsel shall submit to the Hearing Panel of the Board of Ethical Inquiry all other complaints which are not dismissed for the reasons contained herein.

(2) *Formal Hearing.* Formal disciplinary proceedings before a Hearing Panel of the Board of Ethical Inquiry shall be commenced by setting forth the specific charges of misconduct. A copy of such charges shall be served on the respondent and/or the respondent's attorney. In the event

the respondent fails to file an answer within thirty days after service of the charges, it shall be assumed that the respondent does not intend to contest the charge, and the Hearing Panel shall make its decision based solely on the evidence submitted by Counsel. If the respondent files an answer and requests the opportunity to be heard in person, Counsel, after consultation with the Hearing Panel, shall fix the date and place of a hearing, giving the respondent at least fifteen days notice thereof. The notice of hearing shall advise the respondent that the respondent is entitled to be represented by counsel, and to present evidence in his own behalf. Unless the opportunity to appear personally is specifically requested by the respondent or Counsel, there shall be no formal hearing held, and the complaint, defense, and any evidence ("the record") shall be submitted by Counsel to the Hearing Panel by mail. The members of the Hearing Panel may consider the matter by means of personal conference, correspondence, telephone, or other means of communication.

The Hearing Panel shall consist of three voting members of the Board of Ethical Inquiry selected by Counsel, one of whom shall be selected by Counsel to serve as Chairperson. In selecting the members of such a Hearing Panel, Counsel shall be guided by (1) the geographical proximity of the residence of a member to the residence of the respondent and (2) the availability of such member for service. A member so selected shall disclose any fact or circumstance causing him or her to believe that, for a conflict of interests or other meritorious reason, he or she should be disqualified from serving on such Panel. Within thirty days after the conclusion of the hearing, the Hearing Panel shall submit its report to the entire Board of Ethical Inquiry. The report shall summarize the evidence and contain the recommendations of its majority and any minority opinion. The majority vote of all voting members of the Board of Ethical Inquiry voting shall determine the acceptance or rejection of the recommendation of the Hearing Panel.

In those disciplinary matters which must be reviewed by, or which are appealed to, the Ethics Policy Committee ("the Committee"), Counsel shall submit the record, including the decision of the Board of Ethical Inquiry to the

Chairperson of the Committee by mail. The respondent will be conclusively deemed to have waived all objections to the findings and recommendations of the Board of Ethical Inquiry unless the respondent had filed an answer upon service of the initial charges and notice of the institution of formal disciplinary proceedings before a Hearing Panel of the Board of Ethical Inquiry, as provided above. There shall be no formal hearing, and the Committee may make its decision on the record by means of personal conference, correspondence, telephone, or other means of communication. The Committee shall either approve, disapprove, or modify the recommendation of the Board of Ethical Inquiry within thirty days after the submission of the record by Counsel.

C. *Procedure for Disciplinary Proceedings Involving Applicants for the CPCU Program.* Whenever Counsel determines that an applicant for the CPCU Program may have violated the *Code of Professional Ethics*, Counsel shall recommend, after investigation and in accord with the procedures herein, whether or not such applicant shall be approved or rejected.

(1)   In cases where the alleged *Code* violation involves the breach of *Rule R3.3* of the *Code* or the suspension of a business or professional license, but where it appears that the applicant has been fully rehabilitated, Counsel shall secure the concurrence of two members of the Board of Ethical Inquiry before Counsel may authorize the acceptance of such application. If either of such members disagrees with Counsel's recommendation, the matter shall be submitted to a Hearing Panel in the same manner as a disciplinary matter referred to in IV. B. above.

(2)   If the disciplinary matter involves an alleged *Code* violation other than the types described in IV. C. (1) above, and where Counsel, after investigation, determines that the applicant has been fully rehabilitated, counsel shall secure the concurrence of two members of the Management Council of the American Institute for Property and Liability Underwriters before Counsel may authorize the acceptance of such application. If either of such members disagrees with Counsel's recommendation, the matter shall be submitted to a Hearing Panel in the same manner as a disciplinary matter referred to in IV. B. above.

(3)   If, after investigation, Counsel determines that the application should be rejected, Counsel shall advise the

applicant in writing that the application will be submitted to a Hearing Panel of the Board of Ethical Inquiry with the recommendation that it be rejected. If the applicant contests the proposed recommendation, the applicant shall notify Counsel in writing, within thirty days of the receipt of such notice, of the desire to contest the recommendation together with any defense or evidence on the applicant's behalf. Counsel shall then submit the matter to a Hearing Panel in the same manner as a disciplinary matter referred to in IV. B. above. Unless the opportunity to appear personally is specifically requested by the respondent or Counsel, there shall be no formal hearing held, and the complaint, defense, and any evidence ("the record") shall be submitted by Counsel to the Hearing Panel by mail. The members of the Hearing Panel may consider the matter by means of personal conference, correspondence, telephone, or other means of communication. Within thirty days after the conclusion of the hearing, the Hearing Panel shall submit its report to the entire Board of Ethical Inquiry. The report shall summarize the evidence and contain the recommendation of its majority and any minority opinion.

(4)   If the decision of the majority of the Board of Ethical Inquiry is to reject the application, the applicant shall have thirty (30) days within which to request a review of the decision by the Ethics Policy Committee, such review to be considered in the same manner as disciplinary matters referred to in IV. B. (2) above.

D.   *Procedure for Disciplinary Proceedings Involving Candidates for the CPCU Program.* Whenever Counsel determines that a candidate for the CPCU Program may have violated the *Code of Professional Ethics*, Counsel shall recommend, after investigation and in accord with the procedures herein, whether or not such candidate shall be approved or disapproved.

(1)   In cases where the alleged *Code* violation involves the breach of *Rule R3.3* of the *Code* or the suspension of a business or professional license, but where it appears that the candidate has been fully rehabilitated, Counsel shall secure the concurrence of two members of the Board of Ethical Inquiry in the continuation of the candidacy in good standing of such candidate. If either of such members disagrees with Counsel's recommendation, the matter shall be submitted to a Hearing Panel in the same

manner as a disciplinary matter referred to in IV. B. above.

(2) If the disciplinary matter involves an alleged *Code* violation other than the types described in IV. D. (1) above, and where Counsel, after investigation, determines that the candidate has been fully rehabilitated, Counsel shall secure the concurrence of two members of the Management Council of the American Institute for Property and Liability Underwriters in continuation of the candidacy in good standing of such candidate. If either of such members disagrees with Counsel's recommendation, the matter will be submitted to a Hearing Panel in the same manner as a disciplinary matter referred to in IV. B. above.

(3) If, after investigation, Counsel determines that the candidacy in good standing of such candidate should be terminated, Counsel shall advise the candidate in writing that the matter will be submitted to a Hearing Panel of the Board of Ethical Inquiry with the recommendation to terminate the candidacy.

   If the candidate contests the proposed recommendation, the candidate shall notify Counsel in writing, within thirty days of the receipt of such notice, of the desire to contest the recommendation together with any defense or evidence on the candidate's behalf. Counsel shall then submit the matter to a Hearing Panel in the same manner as a disciplinary matter referred to in IV. B. above. Unless the opportunity to appear personally is specifically requested by the respondent or Counsel, there shall be no formal hearing held, and the complaint, defense, and any evidence ("the record") shall be submitted by Counsel to the Hearing Panel by mail. The members of the Hearing Panel may consider the matter by means of personal conference, correspondence, telephone, or other means of communication. Within thirty days after the conclusion of the hearing, the Hearing Panel shall submit its report to the entire Board of Ethical Inquiry. The report shall summarize the evidence and contain the recommendation of its majority and any minority opinion.

(4) If the majority of the Board of Ethical Inquiry rejects the application, the candidate shall have thirty (30) days within which to request a review of the decision by the Ethics Policy Committee. Such review would be considered in the same manner as disciplinary matters referred

to in IV. B. (2) above.

V. Penalties

A. If the Board of Ethical Inquiry determines that a complaint merits disciplinary action, it may impose or recommend, as appropriate, any penalty hereinafter described, *provided* that the severity of the penalty imposed shall be commensurate with the severity of the offense committed. The Board of Ethical Inquiry may also consider all the circumstances surrounding the commission of any offense and the likelihood that the offender has been rehabilitated. All penalties recommended by the Board of Ethical Inquiry must be reviewed, before becoming effective, by the Ethics Policy Committee and approved or modified as appropriate.

B. Penalties which may be administered in appropriate cases are as follows:

(1) with respect to CPCUs subject to the *Code*:

(a) private admonitions, requesting the violator to cease and desist;

(b) reprimands in the form of informal rebukes given limited publication;

(c) censures in the form of formal rebukes given wide publication; and

(d) revocation or suspension of the privilege to use the CPCU designation, for a probationary period or indefinitely, with or without publication.

(2) with respect to CPCU applicants and candidates, admission to any examination may be denied, and awarding of the CPCU designation may be withheld pending receipt of convincing proof of the candidate's full and complete rehabilitation.

C. All proceedings involving allegations of breach of the *Rules of Professional Conduct* shall be kept confidential except as to the parties, but penalties assessed and decisions made may be disclosed, provided the publication of disciplinary sanctions to others shall be approved by the Ethics Policy Committee.

VI. Miscellaneous Provisions

A. (1) Complaints against members of the Board of Ethical Inquiry or Counsel involving alleged violation of the *Rules of Professional Conduct* by them shall be submitted directly to the Ethics Policy Committee.

(2) Complaints against members of the Ethics Policy Com-

mittee involving alleged violations of the *Rules of Professional Conduct* by them shall be submitted directly to the Board of Trustees of the American Institute of Property and Liability Underwriters.

B. Amendments to these Disciplinary Rules, Procedures, and Penalties shall bear their effective date as determined by the Ethics Policy Committee.

Effective 31 August 1976, as amended
17 June 1983, 12 June 1984, and
16 February 1990
Sidney A. Stewart, Jr., CPCU
Chairman
Ethics Policy Committee

ADVISORY OPINIONS
of the
BOARD OF ETHICAL INQUIRY

One of the most important functions of the Board of Ethical Inquiry is to facilitate voluntary compliance with the standards which are set forth in the *Code of Professional Ethics*. Accordingly, the Board periodically publishes *Guidelines* and *Advisory Opinions*. Whenever questions of interpretation arise, CPCUs and CPCU candidates are strongly encouraged to request *Advisory Opinions*. Only the Board of Ethical Inquiry is authorized to issue such opinions on behalf of the American Institute.

Unpublished opinions are informal and intended solely for the guidance of the individuals to whom they are issued, whereas published *Opinions* are formal and intended for the guidance of all persons subject to the *Code*. Each published *Opinion*, except those identified with the prefix "HCS," below, has a specified effective date after which it may be used in interpreting and applying the *Rules of Professional Conduct*. Such effective date for *Opinions HCS-101* through *HCS-122* is 1 June 1978.

Published *Opinions* are presented in the form of the Board's responses to hypothetical case studies. The cases and the corresponding *Opinions*, which are designated by the initials "HCS" and numbered for ease of reference, are "hypothetical" in the sense that they did not arise from actual disciplinary proceedings.* Instead, inquiries of general import are edited, combined, and otherwise fabricated into imaginary case situations in which persons and organizations are referred to by fictitious names. The hypothetical nature of the cases preserves the anonymity of inquirers and provides an efficient means of posing a wide variety of ethical questions and issues to which the *Code*

---

* Unless otherwise noted, hypothetical case studies HCS-112 through HCS-122 assume that the alleged violator *is* bound by the *Rules,* either by voluntary election or by virtue of the CPCU conferment date.

41

may be applied. The Board's *Opinions* anticipate and resolve such questions and issues in advance, thereby helping to prevent conduct which would be unethical and contrary to the public interest.

The Board's published *Opinions* are necessarily based upon abbreviated case summaries and assumptions that are designed to maximize their educational value. It should therefore be obvious that published *Opinions* might differ appreciably from the decisions rendered in actual disciplinary proceedings since the latter decisions would be based upon thorough investigations and hearings of the actual facts, evidence, and circumstances involved. Nonetheless, as official interpretations and applications of the *Rules of Professional Conduct*, the *Opinions* offer useful guidance for CPCUs and CPCU candidates.

CASE HCS-101

Mr. Richard Roe, in completing his matriculation application for the CPCU program, provided complete information regarding his past record of criminal convictions. Further investigation confirmed that Mr. Roe had received his high school diploma in 1950 while confined to a juvenile correctional institution for several counts of shoplifting, disorderly conduct, assaulting his foster parents, and resisting arrest. Within six weeks after his probationary release from the juvenile institution, Mr. Roe was arrested and charged with soliciting for a prostitute and armed robbery. He was convicted on both counts and served ten years in prison. In 1960, after careful consultation with the warden of the state penitentiary, the personnel director of an insurance company hired Mr. Roe to work in the company's printing shop. Seven years later, Mr. Roe, having successfully completed the IIA Program in General Insurance, was promoted to the position of underwriting trainee. He has since advanced to the position of junior underwriter to the "special risks" department and has been promised another promotion if he is able to fulfill the CPCU designation requirements. The personnel director, a CPCU, indicated that he would support Mr. Roe's candidacy. Mr. Roe is now married, forty-seven years of age, and has two children. He is the coach of a little league baseball team and spends two Saturdays each month doing volunteer work at the local home for underprivileged children of deceased parents. Should Mr. Roe's application for the CPCU program be approved? Did the personnel director violate the ethics *Code*? Suppose Mr. Roe had not revealed his criminal record at the time he applied to the Institute, but the Institute discovered the true facts after Roe passed all the exams and met the experience requirements and before the national conferment ceremonies. Should Roe's CPCU designation be conferred?

OPINION HCS-101

Though alleged ethics violations are best interpreted in the context of the entire *Code of Professional Ethics* and related published materials, the standards most directly applicable to the Richard Roe Case are the *Preamble, Rules R3.3* and *R9.1,* and *Guideline G3.4.*

As clearly specified in the *Preamble* to the *Code,* and in the agreements an individual must sign at the time of applying for matriculation into the CPCU program, "all CPCU *candidates* become subject to the binding effect of the *Rules* at the time they matriculate with the American Institute, and thereafter for as long as they remain candidates."

The facts reveal that Mr. Roe had violated the spirit of *Canon 3* and *G3.4* on a number of occasions in the past, both by violating laws and by engaging in activity which caused unjust harm to others. But since no disciplinary action can be taken against any person subject to the *Code*, and in the absence of a *Rule* violation, the issue here is whether Mr. Roe violated *R3.3*. That is to say, do his past criminal violations suggest the likelihood of professional misconduct in the future? Based on the nature and number of crimes committed, the Board feels that the answer must be yes. Mr. Roe did violate *R3.3* and is subject to disciplinary action.

Despite the foregoing, the Board would vote to admit Mr. Roe to CPCU candidacy. The *Preamble* and the published *Disciplinary Rules and Procedures* provide that such action may be taken "upon convincing proof of full and complete rehabilitation." The evidence presented in the hypothetical case, though limited, persuades us to believe that Mr. Roe has been fully rehabilitated, and that he should not be made to suffer the rest of his life for crimes he committed long ago, and for which he has already been punished, as long as he continues to comply strictly with the *Code*.

Had Mr. Roe misrepresented the facts about his criminal record, and had the Institute discovered the misrepresentation before the designation was conferred, the Board would withhold the designation since the misrepresentation would be a violation of *R3.1* and would also be rather strong evidence that he was not fully rehabilitated. Mr. Roe would then be given an opportunity at some later date to offer convincing proof of full rehabilitation. Had Mr. Roe already received the designation, the Board of Ethical Inquiry would recommend to the Ethics Policy Committee that Mr. Roe's privilege to use the designation be suspended.

In the opinion of the Board, the personnel director did not violate *R9.1*. He did initiate and support Mr. Roe's CPCU candidacy, but he had no reason to suspect Roe "to engage in" (at the present time) business practices which violate the *Code*. The personnel director observed the spirit of *G9.2* when he avoided becoming a "self-appointed investigator or judge on matters properly left to the Board" and, we assume, by advising Roe to disclose his criminal record. Moreover, the personnel director seemed to be complying fully with *R5.1* while helping to deal with a serious social problem, jobs for deserving ex-convicts, which the Board thinks is in the spirit of *Canon 1*.

CASE HCS-102

Mr. J. B. White, CPCU, LL.B., is regional claims manager for a large liability insurer. After reviewing a particular property damage liability claim, Mr. White agrees with Alan Adjuster that Mrs. Claimant is justifiably entitled to a settlement of $2,000. However, White instructs Adjuster to offer her $1,200 and a box of good chocolates. "If Mrs. Claimant refuses," White said, "explain to her that if she hires an attorney, his fee will be up to 50 percent of the settlement amount so if she would take our offer she would be $200 ahead of the game. If she still refuses, put the file in your desk drawer for a couple of months. She will eventually see it our way because she really needs the money." Mrs. Claimant later writes to the Board of Ethical Inquiry and argues that White and Adjuster are guilty of ethics violations. Adjuster says he was just following the orders of his superior. White says his action was "in accord with customary industry practices and, anyway, he "did not understand the *Rule of Conduct*, though he had glanced at the Institute's *Code of Professional Ethics* several times." Adjuster is not yet a CPCU, but he has passed the first two of the CPCU examinations.

OPINION HCS-102

It bears repeating that alleged ethics violations are best interpreted in the context of the entire *Code of Professional Ethics* and all the *Guidelines*, *Advisory Opinions*, and *Summaries of Previous Rulings* which have been approved by the Board of Ethical Inquiry and published by the American Institute. However, the standards most directly applicable to the J. B. White—Alan Adjuster Case are those contained in the *Preamble, Rules R1.1, R1.2, R2.1, R3.1, R3.3, R6.1, Guidelines G1.1, G1.2, G1.3, G1.4, G3.4*, and *Canons 1, 3*, and *6*.

Here, as elsewhere, the Board of Ethical Inquiry is empowered to take or recommend disciplinary action only if the accused is (1) subject to the binding effect of the *Rules* and (2) guilty of a *Rule* violation.

Like all other CPCU candidates, Alan Adjuster is clearly bound by the *Rules* of the *Code*. Since he has already passed two of the national CPCU examinations, it is obvious that he is a CPCU "candidate," i.e., that the American Institute had approved his matriculation application and granted him permission to take the examinations. The Institute would not have approved his matriculation application unless he had first signed an agreement to be bound by the ethics and other standards prescribed by the Institute. The applicability of the *Rules* to CPCU candidates is also stipulated in the *Preamble*.

Whether J. B. White is bound by the *Rules* depends upon when his CPCU designation was conferred. He is bound by them automatically if his designation was conferred *after* 18 June 1976, the effective date of the *Code*. But if his designation was conferred *before* 18 June 1976, he is subject to the possibility of disciplinary action only if he voluntarily elects in writing to be bound unconditionally by the mandates of the *Rules* (as explained on page 3 in the *Preamble* to the *Code*). For the purposes of this case, we will assume that Mr. White *is* subject to disciplinary action.

It is the opinion of the Board that both J. B. White and Alan Adjuster have violated several *Rules* of professional conduct. In jurisdictions which have so-called "Unfair Claims Practices Acts," the liability claims settlement approach of White and Adjuster may be contrary to statute and/or regulation, in which case it would be contrary to statute and/or regulation, in which case it would likewise violate *R3.3* of the *Code*. Neither White nor Adjuster would be allowed to plead ignorance of such laws, for the reasons explained in *Guideline G3.4*, since the knowledge of such laws is readily available. Moreover, *Rule R6.1* very explicitly obligates them to "keep informed on the legal limitations imposed upon the scope of (their) professional activities." If the evidence confirmed that White and Adjuster were not aware of an applicable law governing the conduct of claims representatives, that alone would strongly suggest that they are also in violation of the minimum continuing education obligation, which is stipulated in *R2.1* and further clarified in *Guidelines G2.1* through *G2.4*.

Whether or not a statute or regulation had been violated, the Board believes that White and Adjuster did violate *R3.1*. The claims settlement approach in question may or may not meet all the narrow legal tests for "fraud" per se, but in a larger sense the approach is an act of a "dishonest and deceitful" *nature* within the intended meaning of the *Code* provisions since it is tantamount to cheating Mrs. Claimant out of the prompt, equitable, and otherwise fair treatment to which she is ethically entitled. Tactics of delay, bribery, and deliberate underpayment are contrary to the letter of *G1.4*. They clearly caused "unjust harm to others" within the meaning of *Canon 3*. They are flagrantly contrary to the *Canon 6* concept of establishing and maintaining "dignified and honorable relationships with those whom CPCUs serve," and they are clearly contrary to the "public interest" concept which constitutes the most fundamental goal of the entire *Code*, and which is set forth in *Canon 1* and *G1.1* through *G1.4*. While the *Canons and Guidelines* are not themselves enforceable, they can and will be used by the Board in interpreting the *Rules* and applying them to specific factual situations. Here, for instance, they clarify the intended meaning of *R3.1* and support the Board's conclusion that it was violated.

J. B. White's conduct is not excused by either alleged or actual ignorance of the *Code* because *R1.1* clearly gives him "a duty to understand and abide by all the *Rules*" and this is so regardless of whether such *Rules* are violated in practice by others who are not subject to the *Code*. Nor can White's conduct be excused by virtue of his having delegated the actual handling of the claim to Adjuster. White obviously violated *R1.2* by "advocating, sanctioning, participating in, causing to be accomplished, carrying out through another or condoning" an act which White is prohibited from performing under the *Rules*. Alan Adjuster's conduct is likewise in violation of *Rules R3.1, R3.3* and *R6.1*, and *R1.2* makes it clear that such violations are not excused merely because the violator allegedly or actually followed the instructions of his superiors.

Although the members of the Board of Ethical Inquiry agree that both White and Adjuster engaged in conduct which is clearly unethical under the *Code*, additional evidence would be considered before determining the exact nature of the disciplinary actions to be taken. At a minimum, the Board would issue "private admonitions" to White and Adjuster. That is to say, a letter would be sent to each violator. It would notify each that the Board had ruled the conduct to be unethical. It would request each violator to "cease and desist" from engaging in such conduct, and it would forewarn each of the potential consequences of continuing *Rule* violations. If a violator failed to cease and desist, if he was later found guilty of additional violations, or if the original investigation and hearing process disclosed adverse evidence which is not apparent from the limited information given, the Board would probably impose or recommend stronger sanctions. Adjuster, a candidate, could have his CPCU designation withheld, for a probationary period or indefinitely, until such time that he provided convincing proof of his full and complete rehabilitation. J. B. White could be subject to reprimand, censure, or revocation or suspension of the privilege to use the CPCU designation (the latter would have to be approved by the Ethics Policy Committee of the Board of Trustees of the American Institute).

Mrs. Claimant, as a party directly involved, would be notified of the decision and the penalties imposed. She would also be told that the Board has no power to intervene on her behalf in any legal dispute with the insurer. The Board of Ethical Inquiry does have the power, at its discretion, to disclose the decisions and penalties to officers and Chapters of the Society of CPCU, as well as to the parties directly involved. But any publication of sanctions to others, as in a public censure, must first be approved by the Ethics Policy Committee of the Board of Trustees.

CASE HCS-103

Jay Agent, CPCU, and Roger Partner, CPCU, are the owners and operators of a combination real estate and general insurance agency. In recent years Agent has been managing most of the insurance activities, while Partner has concentrated on the real estate portion of the business. Partner bought 500 acres of nearly worthless swampland for $5 an acre, instructed his secretary to run full page ads in various senior citizen publications, eventually sold the land at an average of $4,000 for each half-acre plot, and split the total proceeds with Agent in accordance with the partnership agreement. A retired couple who had purchased one of the plots provided the Institute's Ethics Counsel with evidence that they bought the land only because the advertisement said the subdivision already had paved streets and sidewalks, city water, two swimming pools, tennis courts, a club house, and free lifetime health care for the first twenty couples to buy at least one plot. None of these improvements and benefits were available when they arrived at the swamp with their mobile home. Agent contends that he personally did not violate the *Code* since the insurance aspects of the business were conducted legally and ethically. Partner contends that his real estate activities have nothing to do with insurance, and hence, his status as a CPCU.

OPINION HCS-103

The standards most directly applicable to the Jay Agent—Roger Partner Case are those contained in *Rules R1.1, R1.2, R3.1, R3.2, R3.3, R6.1, Guidelines G1.2, G1.3, G3.3, G3.4,* and *Canons 1, 3,* and *6.* Though not specifically mentioned in the information given, it will be assumed that both Agent and Partner were bound by the *Rules*, either by voluntary election or by virtue of their CPCU conferment dates.

The Board is satisfied that the conduct of Jay Agent and Roger Partner was unethical. First, the evidence would undoubtedly confirm that one or more laws were violated (a breach of *R3.3*), and that the partners should have kept informed on such laws (in accord with *R6.1* and *G3.4*). Furthermore, it is clear that Partner's real estate scheme constituted "an act or omission of a dishonest, deceitful, or fraudulent nature" (thus violating the letter of *R3.1* and the spirit of *Canons 1, 3,* and *6*), that the scheme raises serious questions about possible violations of *R3.2* (as clarified in *G3.3*), and that Agent and Partner have a duty to "*understand* and *abide* by *all* the *Rules*" (as specified in *R1.1,* emphasis supplied). Since there can be little doubt about the foregoing, the real issues here are as follows: Is Partner's real estate scheme outside the purview of the *Code*, as he contends? Does Agent's lack of direct involvement excuse his conduct? What disciplinary actions, if any, should be taken?

Roger Partner's real estate scheme is definitely within the purview of the *Code* and the jurisdiction of the Board. He is a CPCU. He is bound by the *Rules*. And *R3.1* clearly prohibits him from engaging in acts or omissions of a dishonest, deceitful, or fraudulent nature "in the conduct of business or professional activities." It does not say "insurance" activities. It says "business or professional activities," as intended by the drafters of the *Code*, and the phrase most certainly includes real estate activities. Roger Partner is also subject to disciplinary action, under *R3.3*, "for the violation of *any* law or regulation, to the extent *that such violation suggests the likelihood of professional misconduct in the future*" (emphasis supplied). Since the Board is disturbed by the serious nature of the offenses, the consequences to those harmed, and the likelihood of professional misconduct in the future, the Board would recommend that Roger Partner's privilege to use the CPCU designation be suspended indefinitely or revoked. The final decision would be made by the Ethics Policy Committee of the Board of Trustees.

Jay Agent's lack of direct involvement in the real estate scheme does not excuse the fact that he, too, was guilty of *Rule* violations. As stipulated in *R1.2*, "a CPCU shall not advocate, sanction, participate in, cause to be accomplished, otherwise carry out through another, or condone any act which the CPCU is prohibited from performing by the *Rules* of this *Code.*" Even if Agent could prove that he did not advocate or participate in the illegal and fraudulent scheme, there is at least a rebuttable presumption that he "condoned" it by failing to object to the scheme and by accepting his share of the large sum of money involved. Surely a reasonable man would inquire into the source of a $2 million gain. But if Agent did not make such an inquiry, he would probably be guilty of complicity under the law, and he would also surely be in violation of *R3.2* (allowing the pursuit of financial gain to interfere with the exercise of sound professional judgment) and *R4.1* (failing to discharge his occupational duties competently). Accordingly, the Board would recommend to the Ethics Policy Committee that Agent's privilege to use the CPCU designation be suspended indefinitely or revoked.

If the Ethics Policy Committee agreed with the aforementioned recommendations, the decisions would undoubtedly be published widely, as well as conveyed to the complainants. If the final decision was to suspend the privilege to use the designation, both Agent and Partner would be given an opportunity at a later date to offer convincing proof of full and complete rehabilitation.

CASE HCS-104

Bob Broker, CPCU, is the brother of a powerful county politician who arranged for Bob to be broker-of-record on all insurance policies purchased by the county. Though the gross commission Bob receives on this insurance amounts to about $50,000 per year, virtually all of the everyday service work is performed by county and insurance company employees. Bob Broker's role is to place the coverage with the insurers on any cancellation or renewal dates, the coverage having been secured initially by a previous agent. Shortly before the renewal date of one of the policies, Broker obtained premium quotations from two insurers, A and B. Company B quoted a lower price and offered better coverages than Company A, but Broker selected Company A because it paid him a substantially higher commission rate (on a larger total premium). Although never explicitly requested to do so, Bob Broker contributed generously to his brother's political party, frequently entertained county employees on his yacht, and gave his brother the down payment for a new home. Bob's principal competitor, also a CPCU and a broker, reported all this information in a telephone conversation with the Institute's Ethics Counsel, but the competitor indicated that he did not want his name revealed, nor would he testify, in any disciplinary proceedings. He also said that "one of the county's insurers selected by Bob was rumored to be in financial trouble." Any code violations? Suppose a taxpayer brought the charges of ethical impropriety to the Institute.

OPINION HCS-104

In the case of Bob Broker, the first issue to be considered is the refusal of Competitor to testify or have his name used. Since one of the constitutional requirements of "due process" is the right of an accused to be confronted by his accuser(s), the American Institute's *Disciplinary Rules and Procedures* (sections IV. A., B.) provide that "all complaints alleging a violation of the *Code of Professional Ethics shall be submitted in writing to Counsel and signed by the complainant*" (emphasis supplied). If Competitor refused to submit a complaint in writing and sign it, and if no other party was willing to do so, the complaint would be dismissed as frivolous and prima facie without merit. Any person may file a complaint against a CPCU or a CPCU candidate, as long as the complaint complies with the *Disciplinary Rules and Procedures*. However, if Bob Broker received his CPCU designation prior to 18 June 1976 and he had not filed a voluntary written election to be bound by the *Rules*, the case would have to be dismissed for lack of jurisdiction.

Does Competitor's refusal to sign a complaint and testify constitute sufficient grounds for an ethics disciplinary action against him?

While the Board notes with regret that Competitor's attitude is contrary to the aspirational goal of *Canon 9*, there is no basis for a disciplinary action against him because he did not violate a *Rule* per se. *R9.2* does not obligate Competitor to sign a complaint or testify. It only obligates him to reveal, *upon request*, any information he may have concerning an alleged violation of the *Code*. Nor is he obligated to volunteer any information, except in the situation covered by *R9.3* (and clarified in *G9.2*). All CPCUs are encouraged to assist in maintaining the integrity of the *Code*; the reporting of adverse information is enough to prompt an investigation of the matter; the extent of a CPCU's involvement in any disciplinary proceedings is left largely to his or her own judgment; and, the accused is protected from harassment and the deprivation of his rights. Achieving these objectives is a delicate task, perhaps even more so when, as in this case, the complainant is a competitor of the accused.

Assuming that the initial investigation eventually resulted in a proper complaint and sufficient evidence of possible misconduct to justify a formal hearing, the standards most directly applicable to Bob Broker would be *Rules R2.1, R3.1, R3.2, R3.3, R6.1, Guidelines G1.2, G3.1, G3.3, G3.4,* and *Canons 1* and *3*.

It is entirely possible that the political contributions, entertainment, and/or down payment on his brother's home would meet the applicable tests for "rebating" commissions illegally, in which case Broker violated *R3.3* and would be subject to discipline to the extent that the Board feels the violation "suggests the likelihood of professional misconduct in the future." Though the Board obviously will not act solely on the basis of a rumor, if the evidence showed that Broker had recommended an insurer he knew to be in "financial trouble," he clearly violated *R3.1* (a "dishonest, deceitful, or fraudulent act," as clarified in *G3.1*).

If he did not know of the insurer's financial difficulties, it might open the avenue of inquiry into whether Bob Broker had complied with his minimum continuing education obligation under *R2.1*.

Broker's acceptance of commissions for work performed largely by others, though legal on its face, also raises the question of whether he violated the letter of *R3.2* or the spirit of *G1.2* and *G3.3*. The Board acknowledges that the acceptance of such compensation, which is not for and commensurate with services actually rendered or to be rendered, is contrary to the goals of *G1.2* and *G3.3*, but finds no evidence that such acceptance violated *R3.2*. However, the Board feels that Bob Broker probably did violate *R3.2*, as well as *R3.1*, by placing some of the insurance with the insurer who offered higher commissions and lesser coverages. This conclusion is amply supported by *G3.3*, though it obviously assumes that placing the insurance with the other insurer would have better met the consumer's legitimate needs and best interests, the actual determination of which would require additional information.

What disciplinary action, if any, should be taken against Bob Broker? While the investigation and hearings process might well prove to the contrary, it is apparent from the hypothetical facts that Broker may have violated as many as six *Rules* of professional conduct. If he were found guilty on all counts, the Board would recommend suspension of his privilege to use the CPCU designation. If he is found guilty on at least one but not all the counts, a lesser penalty might be imposed, especially if he had not violated any law.

CASE HCS-105

Joe President, CPCU, chief executive officer of a capital stock insurer, made a decision to cancel the agency contracts of all the company's agents in a particular state because of the poor loss ratio on auto insurance business. As a result, thousands of motorists had difficulty securing replacement coverage, and many ended up in the state's assigned risk plan. "My first and most important responsibility is to our stockholders," the president said when asked about the ethical propriety of his decision. "The rates in that state are not adequate to make a profit."

OPINION HCS-105

The standards most directly applicable to the Joe President Case are those contained in *Rules R1.1, R3.1, R3.3, R4.1, R4.2, Guidelines G1.1, G1.2, G1.3, G4.2,* and *Canons 1, 3, 4,* and *6.*

For the purpose of enhancing the educational value of this hypothetical case, the Board has assumed that a proper complaint has been filed, that Joe President is bound by the *Rules*, and that the complaint has alleged violations of the specific *Rules* indicated above. Though the complainant need not be a person directly harmed by the conduct in question, it is reasonable to assume that this particular complaint probably would have been brought by a former agent and/or former policyholder. It is likewise reasonable to assume that Joe President's decision did not violate any law or regulation. If not, there would be no further consideration of *R3.3*, and the inquiry would focus on whether any other ethics *Rule* had been violated.

Despite the fact that the members of the Board share with thousands of others a growing concern about the numerous social issues posed by the role of the automobile in our society, and despite the natural inclination to feel genuine compassion for the agents and policyholders involved in the case, the Board is not empowered to take disciplinary action unless and until a *Rule* has been violated. Nor will the Board allow itself to stretch the *Code* language in an effort to find a convenient scapegoat for social problems far beyond the ability of any one individual to solve. Thus, since the Board finds no evidence of any *Rule* violation, this case would be dismissed on its merits.

In reaching this conclusion, the Board sharply takes issue with Joe President's contention that (his) "first and most important responsibility is to (his) stockholders." True, Joe President's occupational duties make him directly answerable to his Board of Directors and ultimately to the shareholders, and in this case it is probable that he complied with *R4.1* by competently discharging such duties. But his first and most important responsibility as a CPCU is his *ethical* responsibility to understand and abide by the *Rules* of professional conduct. Though his occupational duties would seldom, if ever, be in conflict with the *Rules*, his status as a CPCU makes him answerable to a "higher authority" should a conflict arise. Indeed, that is precisely what distinguishes professional from nonprofessional behavior. For example, it is entirely conceivable that a president could maximize the return to shareholders (at least in the short run) by initiating or condoning criminal or other unlawful activity. It is likewise conceivable that he could maximize short-run returns through conduct which is legal but prohibited under the *Code of Professional Ethics*. In either case, he would be subject to disciplinary action on ethics grounds.

What "excused" Joe President's conduct in this case was *not* that his "first responsibility is to his shareholders," but rather that he did not violate any ethics *Rules*. His decision to cancel the agency contracts was not "dishonest, deceitful, or fraudulent" (*R3.3*), and there is no evidence that Joe President failed to support the kinds of improvements called for in *R4.2* and *G4.2*. Some might argue that his decision was contrary to the aspirational goals of *Canon 1* (serving the public interest) and *Canon 3* (avoiding unjust harm to others). So also could it be argued that President failed to maintain dignified and honorable relationships with agents and policyholders (in accord with the spirit of *Canon 6*). Yet, it could just as well be argued that the spirit of these three *Canons* would have been more seriously breached if the company had continued to do business in that state at the permitted rate levels, and then become financially insolvent. However persuasive such arguments might be, they are not sufficient to support an ethics disciplinary action in the absence of a *Rule* violation.

The Board hopes that Joe President will join with all other insurance professionals in an earnest effort to find satisfactory solutions to the kinds of complex problems reflected in the case. In the meantime, without condoning Joe President's decision, the Board does not feel an ethics disciplinary action against Joe President would provide such a solution. Nor would it otherwise be justified under the *Code*.

CASE HCS-106

Ms. Polly Browne, CPCU, is director of advertising and public relations for a large insurer specializing in individual health insurance. Ms. Browne approved copy for various media advertisements which said "we will write health insurance for you even if you are sick or disabled or have been turned down by other insurers. . .in fact, we will write health insurance for anyone, regardless of age or health." A competitor insurer accuses Ms. Browne of *Code* violations because the ad did not specify that the insurance in question always contains a very restrictive exclusion for "preexisting conditions."

OPINION HCS-106

The Polly Browne Case could involve violations of laws or regulations governing deceptive advertising and thus, the application of *R3.3*. However, since the primary educational objective of the case is to clarify the extent to which the *Code* goes beyond the law, the *Opinion* will focus on the standards contained in *Rules R3.1, R7.2, Guidelines G3.1, G7.4,* and *Canons 3* and *7*.

In the absence of evidence to the contrary, the Board would like to presume that Ms. Browne did not intend to defraud anyone. If not, the question which still remains is whether her approval of the advertising copy constituted an "omission of a dishonest or deceitful nature" (under *R3.1*) and/or a misrepresentation of the "limitations of. . .any product— of an insurer" (under *R7.2*). Though *G3.1* leaves the matter of how much information should be volunteered partially up to Ms. Browne's professional judgment, it also reminds her not to conceal facts which are material to determining the limitations of an insurance contract. And *G7.4* explicitly instructs her not to engage in deceptive advertising practices which significantly mislead the public. Taking all these standards together, and mindful of the spirit of *Canons 3* and *7*, the Board feels Ms. Browne violated both of the applicable *Rules*. As a practical matter, advertising copy cannot be expected to list all of the exclusions and limitations of an insurance contract offered for sale. But in this case there can be little doubt that the public would be significantly misled by the failure to at least mention the preexisting conditions exclusion since the copy itself strongly suggests otherwise.

The Board would probably issue an informal admonition requesting Polly Browne to cease and desist, i.e., to alter the advertising copy so as to conform to the letter and spirit of the *Code*. Stronger sanctions would be imposed only if she failed to comply with the Board's request. The Board believes that comparatively mild disciplinary action is appropriate in this case, but not because the advertising practice in question is fairly common in some segments of the industry. Instead, the action is an acknowledgment of the inherent difficulties posed by the very nature of advertising in contemporary society. If Company A is said to have "the best soap in the world," is this mere "puffing" or is it outright deception? To what extent should the consumer rely upon representations made in advertising? To what extent should the consumer expect advertising to supply all the information needed to make a purchasing decision? That the courts and legislators have struggled with questions such as these is understandable. The issues are formidable in their own right, all the more so when the product is a necessarily complex legal contract like health insurance. Consequently, the Board sees no good reason to impose a harsh penalty on Polly Browne. Unless she blatantly disregards the Board's initial admonitions, it seems enough to remind her that her *Code* obligations require more than obedience to the letter of the law. The Board will not shrink from its responsibility to discipline *Rule* violators, but neither will it allow a preoccupation with discipline to obscure the larger goal of effecting voluntary compliance with the prescribed ethical norms.

CASE HCS-107

Charles Consultant, CPCU, operates his own small insurance consulting business solely in a state which does not require him to be licensed either as a consultant, agent, or broker. Mr. Consultant has extensive business insurance experience and is highly regarded by the corporate clients for whom he consults. He charges all consulting clients a fee of $100 per hour (plus expenses) for his services, which consist largely of drawing up bid specifications for various kinds of insurance, soliciting competitive bids, analyzing the bid proposals, and making recommendations to the client-buyer. Consultant does not recommend agents or brokers per se. Instead, he leaves it up to the buyer to decide whether he is to solicit bids from agents and brokers specified by the buyer or advertise openly for bids from any interested party. For one large corporate client, Mr. Consultant recommends that the client discontinue a particular insurance policy at its renewal date, replace it with aggregate and specific excess-of-loss coverage with large deductibles, and handle the underlying loss exposure with a carefully planned program of funded retention. He also recommends that the client study the feasibility of forming or acquiring its own captive insurer. A local agent alleges that Consultant is guilty of highly unethical conduct because "he always recommends self-insurance, his fees are too high, and he is not even a licensed agent or a member of the agents' association." A second agent objects to what he calls the "unfair competition of Consultant allowing only selected agents to bid for the better client-buyers." And a third agent challenges the ethics of "competitive bidding for private corporations and always recommending to them the lowest priced bid."

OPINION HCS-107

The standards which might apply most directly to the Charles Consultant case are those contained in *Rules R3.2, R4.1, R7.1, R7.2, Guidelines G3.3, G7.5,* and *Canon 3, 4,* and *7.* However, since there is no evidence that any *Rules* were violated by Consultant, the case would be dismissed on its merits.

Despite the unsupported allegations of the three local agents, the law does not require Consultant to be licensed or to join the agents' association, and there is nothing in his conduct, bidding procedures, or recommendations which would violate laws, regulations, or other standards in the ethics *Code*. To the contrary, Consultant appears to be competently and consistently discharging his duties in full compliance with *R4.1*. Recommendations concerning deductibles, funded retention, and the feasibility of captive insurers may even be ethically required in given factual situations where they best serve the client's interests, by the dictates of *Rules R7.1, R7.2,* and *G7.5*. Such recommendations are certainly not ipso facto unethical in the present case. If Consultant *always* recommended self-insurance and/or the lowest priced bid, as was alleged, it would raise questions about both his competence and his ethics. But the Board finds no evidence to support these allegations.

Nor does the Board see anything unethical about the size of Consultant's hourly fee. We assume that the employer-clients agreed in advance to pay Consultant $100 per hour for agreed-upon services, and that he actually delivered those services. Thus, whether the fee was $100 or $1,000 per hour, it was neither "at the expense of the uninformed" nor "unconscionable" within the meaning of *G3.3*, nor did it violate *R3.2* because the evidence suggests that Consultant's recommendations were in the best interests of his clients. He did not allow the pursuit of financial gain to interfere with the exercise of his sound professional judgment and skills.

The Board will not apply *R3.2* to sit in judgment of the level of compensation a CPCU receives in the marketplace for his or her services since it is not the absolute level of compensation which makes professional services ethically suspect. It is whether the pursuit of any amount of financial gain clouded the judgment of the professional, i.e., seduced him to make judgments which were not in the best interests of those served that makes professional services suspect. The purpose of *R3.2* is to prohibit the CPCU from doing something analogous to the surgeon who, in pursuit of a fee, performs surgery that is neither necessary nor desirable for the patient. The surgeon's professional peers would undoubtedly regard his conduct as unethical, whether the fee was $50 for $5,000 because it was the act of performing the surgery that was unethical. The fee was merely the inducement.

CASE HCS-108

Howard Johnson, CPCU, has been a casualty underwriter for thirty-five years. He received his designation in 1958 when he was enthusiastic about insurance education and felt that the designation would help him in his climb up the corporate ladder. Having been "locked in to a dead-end job" for the past five years with no hope of breaking out, his attitude toward continuing education has changed. He has dropped out of a local CPCU chapter, refuses to attend meetings of any kind, discourages fellow employees from seeking the designation, and is anxiously awaiting retirement. His job performance is acceptable in every respect. He has *not* signed an election to be bound by the *Rules* of the *Code*. Nevertheless, the president of the local CPCU chapter requests that the Board of Ethical Inquiry take appropriate action under *R2.1* and *R5.2*.

OPINION HCS-108

The case of Howard Johnson would have to be dismissed for lack of jurisdiction. Since Johnson received his CPCU designation prior to 18 June 1976, and since he did not file a voluntary written election to be bound by the *Rules*, the Board has no authority to take any disciplinary action against him (as specified in the *Preamble* and reaffirmed in *Opinion HCS-102*).

Had Johnson been subject to the binding effect of the *Rules*, he would probably be disciplined by admonishment, reprimand, or even censure for clear-cut violations of *R5.2*. That *Rule* would not obligate him to encourage everyone to pursue CPCU studies, but it would obligate him to encourage and assist *those who wish to pursue* CPCU or other studies, in keeping with the spirit of *Canon 5*. Johnson's attitude toward continuing education would also justify a determination of whether he had violated his own continuing education obligation under *R2.1* and the related *Guidelines*.

CASE HCS-109

Jack Fieldman, CPCU, a field representative of a small multiline insurer, is making a sales presentation with an agent who is not a CPCU. Acquiring the account would greatly enhance Jack's position with his company because it is a prestigious account and a sales campaign is in progress. Part of the proposal is a business package policy with a $1,000 deductible applicable to the property coverages.

In his zeal to make the sale, Jack fails to disclose the deductible. He feels no guilt because he knows that many of his competitors do not mention deductibles unless specifically asked by the applicant or insured.

If a complaint is received from the insured, should any disciplinary action be taken against Fieldman?

OPINION HCS-109

The standards most directly applicable to the Jack Fieldman Case are those contained in *Rules R3.1* and *R7.2, Guidelines G3.1*, and *Canons 3* and *7*.

Since it does not appear that Fieldman was guilty of a "misrepresentation" within the meaning of *R7.2*, the issue turns on whether his failure to disclose a policy provision constituted a violation of *R3.1*. Specifically, was his nondisclosure an "omission of a dishonest, deceitful, or fraudulent nature?"

Guideline G3.1 illustrates the general kinds of acts and omissions which can violate *R3.1*, and which normally "would cause unjust harm to others," thus violating the spirit of *Canon 3*. The *Guideline* explicitly stipulates, "A CPCU should neither misrepresent nor *conceal* a fact or information which is material to determining the . . . scope or *limitations* of . . . an insurance contract" (emphasis supplied). However, the *Guideline* goes on to say, ". . . the extent to which a CPCU should volunteer information and facts must necessarily be left to sound professional judgments of what is required under the circumstances."

Clearly, the drafters of the *Code* did not intend to treat every omission as though it were dishonest, deceitful, or fraudulent if only because it would be so obviously unrealistic to require CPCUs to give every prospective purchaser a full-scale educational course on every insurance contract under consideration. But it also seems clear, from all the relevant standards taken together, that an omission would violate *R3.1* if, based on sound professional judgment, the voluntary disclosure of facts or information is required by the circumstances because the disclosure is (1) material to the buyer's decision making and (2) necessary to avoid what would otherwise cause unjust harm to others.

This type of nondisclosure may be common among his competitors, as Jack contends, but his ethical obligations are prescribed by the *Code* and not by the conduct of others. The Board believes Jack Fieldman did violate *R3.1*, that he was aware of his ethical obligations under the *Rule*, and that he felt himself to be excused by the practices of others (many of whom are not subject to the *Code*). The Board would at least issue a private admonition requesting Fieldman to cease and desist, and the disciplinary penalty might be more severe if there was sufficient evidence of fraud and/or if the insured had been significantly harmed. In any event, the insured would be reminded that the Board's action under the *Code* is independent of any remedies the insured may have at law.

CASE HCS-110

Ann Underwriter, CPCU, is an auto underwriter with the Fire and Casualty Company. Her job includes the selection and rejection of applicants for auto insurance and requires that she make a decision regarding the class into which the applicant will be placed. All applicants are categorized as above average, or below average, and the premium charged is considerably higher for below average insureds.

One of the agents in her territory is Sue Agent, who also runs a foreign car agency. Sue's business is dominated by members of one ethnic group who live in a section of the city that is somewhat rundown, but there are no available data to indicate a higher-than-average loss ratio in that area. Ann has automatically classed these applicants as below average because she believes that they are "bad risks." Has Ann violated the ethics *Code*?

OPINION HCS-110

In most jurisdictions, underwriting practices predicated upon the ethnic origin of the applicant (or insured) would be unlawful discrimination under applicable state and federal statutes and regulations. Therefore, the practice of Ann Underwriter would likewise be a violation of *R3.3* under the *Code*, and she would be subject to disciplinary action to the extent that her violation "suggests the likelihood of professional misconduct in the future." If she attempted to plead ignorance of the applicable law, she would be acknowledging that she also violated *R2.1* and *R6.1*. An underwriter who is not familiar with antidiscrimination laws is violating her duty to "keep informed on those technical matters that are essential to the maintenance of (her) professional competence," as well as her duty to "keep informed on the legal limitations imposed upon the scope of (her) professional activities."

Assuming Ann Underwiter did violate one or more *Rules*, she would at least be issued an informal admonition to cease and desist. And she would be forewarned that any additional *Rule* violation will subject her to the possibility of more severe penalties.

If Ann Underwriter did not in fact violate any law or regulation, on the other hand, the case would be dismissed on its merits. Perhaps her conduct would have been contrary to the spirit of several *Canons* and *Guidelines*, but it would not have breached any *Rule*. The drafters of the *Code* chose not to include an ethics *Rule* on discrimination per se in recognition of the fact that the very process of pooling involves certain types of lawful "discrimination" as an actuarial necessity, and certain types of "discrimination" are also required by law as a matter of rating equity. Thus, a CPCU will not be guilty of an ethics violation for discrimination unless (1) it is unlawful discrimination (which would be a breach of *R3.3*) or (2) the discrimination itself is lawful but otherwise involves an act or omission prohibited by the *Rules*.

CASE HCS-111

A CPCU who is a loss prevention engineer employed by an insurance company feels that an insured firm is engaging in practices which violate many of the requirements of the Occupational Safety and Health Act (OSHA). The CPCU reports these violations to the insurer's underwriting department but not to the Occupational Safety and Health Administration.

To what extent, if any, is the CPCU subject to discipline under the *Code*?

OPINION HCS-111

Under certain circumstances, the Engineer Case might involve violations of laws or regulations (and thus, the application of *R3.3* as well as related *Rules* and *Guidelines*). However, in keeping with the educational objective of the case, the *Opinion* will focus on the standards contained in *Rules R4.1, R5.4, R6.2, R7.2, Guidelines G4.7, G6.6, G7.2,* and *Canons 6* and *7*.

We will assume that a proper complaint has been brought and that Engineer is subject to the binding effect of the *Rules*. It is also reasonable to assume that Engineer informed the insured firm of the practices which he felt were not in compliance with OSHA, in which case Engineer did not violate *R7.2* or the spirit of *G7.2* and *Canon 7*. Had Engineer represented that the firm was in full compliance with OSHA, he would have violated *R3.1* (by committing, in the conduct of his professional activities, an act of a dishonest nature). In fact, even if the firm appeared to be in full compliance with OSHA, Engineer should make clear to the insured firm that this is merely a professional opinion; otherwise, he would run the danger of violating *R7.2* ("A CPCU shall not misrepresent. . .the limitations of any. . .service of an insurer.")

By disclosing this information to his underwriting department, Engineer did not violate *R6.2* since such disclosure is specifically permitted when "made to a person who necessarily must have the information in order to discharge legitimate occupational or professional duties." Indeed, in this case, Engineer's disclosure to underwriting is consistent with his *R4.1* duty (to) "competently. . .discharge (his own) occupational duties." Furthermore, Engineer's failure to report the firm's practices to OSHA does not violate *R5.4*. The latter *Rule* does not obligate him to volunteer information. It only obligates him to disclose information *officially requested by appropriate regulatory authorities*, and then only regarding laws governing the qualifications or conduct of *insurance practitioners*.

Since we have assumed that no law or regulation was violated by Engineer, and since no other *Rules* of the *Code* were breached, the case would be dismissed on its merits.

Unless otherwise noted, all the remaining hypothetical case studies assume that the alleged violator *is* bound by the *Rules*, either by voluntary election or by virtue of the CPCU conferment date.

CASE HCS-112

A CPCU who is a full-time risk manager regularly renews his employer's insurance with the same insurers year after year, refusing insurance agents' requests for specifications to be used for competitive bids. The CPCU's refusal is based on an honest, but mistaken, belief that the insurance the company now carries provides the best available coverage and claim service at the lowest available cost. No complaint has been filed with the Board of Ethical Inquiry (BEI).

Is this CPCU "subject to discipline" for violation of the *Code*? May the agent, who is a CPCU candidate, call the matter to the attention of the Board of Ethical Inquiry? If so, what are the required procedures?

OPINION HCS-112

To clarify the procedural question, suppose a member of the BEI read in the newspaper about a person who had been indicted for embezzlement. The member just happened to know that the indicted person is a CPCU. This kind of situation obviously would prompt an investigation at the Board's own initiative. However, the Board is usually not aware of an alleged *Code* violation unless and until someone voluntarily reports it to the Ethics Counsel. Any person may report an alleged violation. So also may any person file a formal complaint as long as the complaint is in compliance with the American Institute's published *Disciplinary Rules and Procedures*.

In the Risk Manager Case, let us suppose that the agent reported an alleged *Rule* violation. Unless the agent signed a written complaint, or his informal oral report prompted an investigation which later revealed sufficient evidence of a possible *Rule* violation, the case would be dismissed as frivolous and prima facie without merit. Thus, to preserve the educational value of the case, we will assume that Risk Manager has been appropriately accused of violating *Rule R4.1* and the spirit of *Canon 4*.

Rule R4.1 stipulates, "A CPCU shall competently and consistently discharge his or her occupational duties." Nonetheless, *Guideline G4.1* makes it clear that ". . .the Board will not intervene nor arbitrate between the parties in an employment or contractual relationship. . . . Nor does the Board feel that the Institute's disciplinary procedures should become a substitute for legal and other remedies available to such parties. In the event of an alleged violation of *Rule R4.1*, therefore, the Board will hear the case only after all other remedies have been exhausted. . . ." As an employee, Risk Manager has an employment relationship with his employer-firm. His employer is the primary party to whom his occupational duties are owed. If the risk manager is guilty of failing to discharge his occupational duties competently and consistently, the employer may dismiss him and/or take other appropriate actions. If no such actions are taken by the employer or other affected parties (e.g., the stockholders), the BEI will not hear the case.

Furthermore, *G4.1* goes on to say that, even when all other remedies have been exhausted, the Board will take disciplinary action "only under circumstances where (1) a proven violation has caused unjust harm to another *person* and the violation brings substantial discredit upon the CPCU designation; or (2) it would otherwise be in the *public* interest to take disciplinary action under the ethics code" (emphasis supplied). Since there is no evidence that either of these two criteria are met in the hypothetical case, the Board would not take disciplinary action under *R4.1*. By renewing his firm's insurance with the same insurers year after year, the risk manager may be acting with admirable competence, particularly under tight market conditions. Or, the facts may reveal a human error in judgment, an error of the type which even the most competent professional can make, which would not in itself violate the *Rule*. Even if the facts support a finding of incompetence on the part of Risk Manager, the other (*G4.1*) prerequisites of disciplinary action are not met in this case. The only basis of disciplinary action against Risk Manager is that he may have violated *R2.1* (i.e., he may have failed to keep informed on those matters which are essential to the maintenance of his professional competence as a risk manager). As indicated in *G2.3*, "if a CPCU is accused of violating any other *Rule* in the *Code*, the Board may, at its discretion, require the accused to furnish evidence of compliance with *Rule 2.1*." Such evidence of compliance is especially likely to be sought in cases involving allegations of incompetence.

Finally, it should be noted that the rationale of *G4.1* is not limited to cases involving the employer-employee relationship per se. It applies to *any* alleged violation of *R4.1*, i.e., to any case where a CPCU (or CPCU candidate) is accused of failing to discharge his or her occupational duties competently and consistently. The Board will not hear the case unless and until all other available remedies have been exhausted.

CASE HCS-113

A CPCU who is an agent is negotiating manuscript products liability coverage with an insurance company underwriter. He doubts that the underwriter is aware that the Consumer Product Safety Commission (CPSC) is considering investigating the safety of one of his client's products. An unfavorable finding by the Commission is likely to force the client-company to incur large product recall expenses, which will be covered by the policy being negotiated if it is issued. The agent does not mention to the underwriter this possible action by the Commission, and the underwriter does not ask about any such action.

To what extent, if any, is this CPSU subject to discipline under the *Code*? If the CPCU was a broker instead of an agent, would this be material to the findings of the Board?

OPINION HCS-113

While it is true that Agent has a contractual relationship with his insurer-principal, we assume he was not accused of violating *R4.1*; hence, the Board may hear the case, apart from any remedies which may be available to the insurer.

The real issue here is whether Agent violated his *R3.1* duty by engaging in "any act or omission of a dishonest, deceitful, or fraudulent nature." Generally speaking, since underwriting techniques and requirements vary considerably among insurers, the Board believes it would be unreasonable to expect an agent to know every kind of information a particular underwriter would deem material to the writing of a particular kind of insurance. Thus, the Board sees no ethical reason for an agent to volunteer information in his possession *except* when (1) the information is specifically requested in the application, (2) the information is specifically requested by the underwriter or other authorized employee of the insurer, *OR* (3) the agent knows that the information is material to most insurers writing the kind of insurance in question, and the agent has good reason to believe the insurer cannot readily discover the information through inspection or other commonly used sources of underwriting information. (That he should know these things is reinforced by *R2.1*.) As indicated in *G3.1*, "the extent to which a CPCU should volunteer information and facts necessarily must be left to sound professional judgments of what is required under the circumstances." The above three criteria are provided to assist agent-CPCUs in making sound professional judgments about the disclosure of information to underwriters.

In this case, Agent surely knew that a pending CPSC investigation would be "material" to any of the few insurers who write products recall coverage, i.e., he at least should have known that the information might well effect the insurer's underwriting decision or the pricing of the insurance. He, therefore, was guilty of concealing a material fact, ethically if not legally.

He violated *R3.1* by engaging in an omission of a dishonest or deceitful nature (whether the omission was also fraudulent would depend upon his intent). In the absence of evidence to the contrary, it can be inferred that he also might have violated *R3.2* by "allowing the pursuit of financial gain. . .to interfere with the exercise of sound professional judgment and skills." The Board would reprimand the agent in the form of an informal rebuke given limited publication. If there was satisfactory evidence of fraud, the Board would recommend public censure or suspension of the privilege to use the CPCU designation, and the final decision would be made by the Ethics Policy Committee of the American Institute's Board of Trustees.

The same conclusion would essentially be reached if the accused had been a broker instead of an agent. True, in most states an agent is legally a representative of the insurer, whereas the broker is a representative of the applicant or insured. The legal duties of the two may differ somewhat. But the ethical duties under the *Code* do not. Both have ethical duties to their clients, and both are summoned by *Canon 1* to put the public interest above their own. *Guideline G1.2* acknowledges apparent or real conflicts of interest. Yet, it also reminds us that the *public* interest is best served by strict compliance to the prescribed *Rules* of ethical conduct. We cannot believe that an agent's knowing concealment from an insurer of a material fact is in the public interest. And the ethics of any act or omission remain the same regardless of whether or not the action is committed by a broker or an agent.

CASE HCS-114

A CPCU who is a risk manager has purchased for his firm, in the nonadmitted market, an insurance coverage which the risk manager knows is available in the admitted market, but at a higher premium than the nonadmitted coverage. The CPCU knows that the broker through whom the nonadmitted coverage was purchased did not comply with the applicable surplus lines law. Has the risk manager violated any *Rules* under the *Code*?

OPINION HCS-114

Though most surplus lines laws contain a number of specific exemptions which might excuse the conduct of the broker and the risk manager, the Board will assume as fact that the broker did violate the applicable law. The Board has no jurisdiction over the broker since he is not a CPCU or CPCU candidate. The question is whether the CPCU risk manager has violated any *Rules* of the ethics *Code*.

Despite the fact that the risk manager did not directly violate a law or regulation (and therefore is not subject to discipline under *R3.3*), he did violate his *R1.2* duty. He may not literally have "advocated or sanctioned" the broker's conduct. But he did "otherwise carry out through another or condone" an act (violating the law) which he himself is prohibited from performing by the *Rules* of the ethics *Code*. The risk manager would be informally admonished for unethical conduct and given a reasonable length of time to make satisfactory insurance arrangements for his firm. In some states, for example, he might be able to obtain the Commissioner's approval of an arrangement which would, in the absence of such approval, violate the surplus lines law. If he could not do so, he would be ethically obligated to place the insurance with an authorized insurer, even if it meant higher premiums for his employer firm because that is what is required by the typical law. A particular law may appear to be unreasonable or unfair, but that does not leave a CPCU free to violate it, either directly or through another. Nor does the fact that a law penalizes his employer excuse a CPCU for violating *R1.2* of the *Code*. A CPCU's first ethical obligation is to serve the public interest by strict compliance with all the *Code Rules* (see *G1.2*).

The risk manager would not be obligated by *R5.4* to report the broker's law violation unless the risk manager had been properly subpoenaed by the appropriate regulatory authorities in the process of investigating or prosecuting the broker's alleged violation of the insurance laws. In fact, as a practical matter, this particular case might never be brought to the attention of the Board of Ethical Inquiry. It is conceivable that a Commissioner or an authorized insurer would be willing to register an ethics complaint. But the broker or employer-policyholder surely would not. The case is no less valuable as an educational tool, nonetheless, in keeping with the Board's desire to foster and encourage voluntary compliance with the prescribed ethical norms. Furthermore, suppose a case with essentially the same facts involved two CPCUs who are brokers in competition for the risk manager's account, and assume that one broker had secured the account with a lower premium proposal from an unauthorized insurer, in violation of the surplus lines law. Realistically, a competitor broker, having been harmed, is more likely to file an ethics complaint with the Board.

CASE HCS-115

John Manager, CPA, CPCU, is the treasurer of a large insurance company. In order to induce Brown, a potential investor, to purchase a substantial portion of its new bond issue, Manager intentionally certified the financial status of XYZ Corporation, the manufacturer of fire fighting equipment, as sound. In fact, Manager knew the XYZ Corporation was nearly insolvent, but he was persuaded to do so by his brother-in-law, the president of XYZ Corporation, in the honest belief that without the successful sale of the bond issue several hundred employees of XYZ would lose their jobs.

After the bonds had been purchased by Brown, the scheme was discovered and Manager, in addition to criminal penalties, was disciplined by the State Institute of Certified Public Accountants.

Is Manager subject to disciplinary action under the CPCU ethics *Code* if it can be shown by proper evidence that:

(a)   he personally and financially benefited from his illegal act?

   OR

(b)   he was solely motivated by his concern for the jobs involved and no one has sustained any loss in consequence of his act?

   OR

(c)   XYZ Corporation was not a manufacturer, but a large insurance brokerage firm; otherwise, the facts are the same as in (b)?

OPINION HCS-115

It is quite clear that John Manager violated his *R3.1* duty by engaging in an "act or omission of a dishonest, deceitful or fraudulent nature." Since this *Rule* applies to any "business or professional activities," it would not matter that the XYZ Corporation was an insurance brokerage firm or a manufacturer, as asked in hypothetical question (c). It is a *Rule* violation in either case.

Manager also violated the security laws. He is therefore subject to disciplinary action under *R3.3*, as further clarified under *G3.4*, "to the extent that such violation suggests the likelihood of professional misconduct in the future." If Manager financially benefited from his act, as suggested in hypothetical question (a), he also violated *R3.2* (by allowing the pursuit of financial gain to interfere with the exercise of sound professional judgments and skills). In view of the gravity of the three *Rule* violations, the Board would recommend suspension of the privilege to use the CPCU designation. If the Ethics Policy Committee concurred with the recommendation, the suspension would remain in effect until such time that Manager could provide convincing proof of full and complete rehabilitation.

Hypothetical question (b) slightly changes the circumstances by assuming that Manager was motivated solely by an altruistic concern for the employees and that no one sustained any loss as a consequence of his act. His motivations do not alter the conclusion that he violated *Rules* of the *Code*. However, a violator's motivations may be taken into consideration, along with other factors, in determining the severity of the penalty to be imposed.

CASE HCS-116

A CPCU making calls in a community is reviewing an insurance portfolio with a prospective new client (gas station operator) and finds a garage liability policy that expired forty-five days ago. With it is a thirty-day binder and a cover letter from the present agent saying that the renewal policy should be mailed within ten days. Nothing has been received in the interim. The new agent says, "The cold, hard facts are that you have no proof of coverage at all, and if you were sued because of an injury here on the premises or arising out of the operation of your car or wrecker, you might find yourself high and dry. This isn't to say that you couldn't eventually recover the damages from the insurance company or the agent, but it might be very difficult for you to do it—and it might cost you a lot in terms of time and legal expense. It appears that your agent has mishandled your account, and I recommend that you get new coverage into effect immediately. I can leave a written binder with you right now and will have the new policy back here within ten days." The gas station operator said, "OK, let's do it!" The former agent learned of this discussion two weeks later when he delivered the "renewal policy." He now contends that the CPCU's action was unethical and that the situation demanded a telephone call to find out whether a "current binder" was in effect. A formal complaint is filed with the Ethics Counsel of the Institute, after which it becomes known that a member of the Board of Ethical Inquiry is a competitor of the CPCU being charged with an ethics violation. The CPCU being charged lives over 2,000 miles from Malvern, PA.

OPINION HCS-116

The CPCU's conversation with a client suggests the possibility that a competitor may eventually bring a legal action for slanderous defamation of character, which would be a matter for the courts to decide. There also might be a basis for contending that the CPCU's conduct was contrary to the spirit of *Canon 6* and *Guidelines G6.1* and *G6.2* (which summon a CPCU to strive for dignified and honorable relationships with competitors). Against this it can be argued that his conduct did not cause "*unjust* harm to others" within the meaning of *Canon 3*. Vigorous competition is often in the public interest, and it is not inherently unethical to offer improvements in a prospective client's insurance arrangements. Indeed, an agent who did not do so ordinarily would be violating his *R4.1* obligation to discharge his occupational duties competently. A dignified and honorable professional does not make a habit of criticizing his competitors in a personal manner. Yet, whenever an insurance advisor convinces a client of the need to effect improvements in existing insurance arrangements, a need which is not infrequent, there is nothing to keep the client from drawing the inference that his previous advisers were careless or incompetent. Clearly, a client can benefit from a particular agent's knowledge, skill, and diligence. And the Board sees no ethical reason why such an agent should be required to telephone or otherwise share with his competitor a lawful and desirable trade advantage which he has obtained through his own efforts. Whatever the merits of these arguments may be, the Board is not empowered to take disciplinary action unless a *Rule* of the *Code* has been violated.

Given the brief description of the hypothetical case, about the only *Rule* which might be applicable is *R3.1* (which imposes a duty to refrain from allowing the pursuit of financial gain to interfere with the exercise of sound professional judgment), and it should be interpreted within the context of *Canon 3*. The CPCU's use of words like "mishandled your account" borders on the indiscreet. But the Board finds no persuasive evidence of unsound professional judgment which would cause unjust harm to others. Accordingly, the case would be dismissed on its merits.

If the case had progressed to the stage of a hearing, the initial hearing would be held in the geographical proximity of the accused so as to minimize travel expenses. And a member of the BEI is obligated to disqualify himself or herself if serving on the hearing panel would involve a potential conflict of interest (e.g., serving as a judge of a competitor).

CASE HCS-117

A CPCU who is a part-time university professor decided to run a Saturday morning CPCU 1 class from 8:00 A.M. to noon, on the first Saturday in the month. When the local chapter people heard of the plan, they contacted him to discuss two aspects of such a plan:

1. the educational feasibility of such a plan in the light of their past experiences with "doubled up" classes; and

2. the fact that it would be "in competition" with their own plans for CPCU 1 on Tuesday evenings.

The professor dismissed the first point of discussion by noting that he had previously run a Naval Reserve Class of "Confidential Document Classification" on exactly the same basis and that it had been very successful. If it could work there, it certainly could work with CPCU. On the second point, he was confident that the people he would get on Saturday morning would be persons who would not be coming to the Tuesday night class anyway since "agents are always out making calls in the evening."

The chapter people called the Institute to see "what could be done about this situation." An Institute staff member called the professor to discuss the potential educational pitfalls in the four-to-five-topics-in-one-day-a-month approach, and told him of unsuccessful efforts in that direction in other communities. Professor indicated that since he already had thirty students who had submitted their $200, he felt obligated to proceed with the plan. Contact with the professor through the year revealed that the chapter/Institute predictions of attrition, nonpreparation, no exam practice, and so on, were being fulfilled as early as the November and December meetings. At the end of the year the roster sheet report to the professor revealed a course effectiveness ratio that was approximately one-third that of the national average. Concurrent with the receipt of the roster sheet feedback, the chapter president called again to say that a mailing had gone out again announcing another CPCU 1 class offering on the same basis. Their call to the professor led to his statement that "while there had been some problems with the group, I don't see any justification for concluding that it was the format that was the problem."

Yet another conversation with the professor was held by conference call with two Institute staff members, but the professor was not to be dissuaded. The fee had gone to $250 and the professor felt that there was a real interest and demand for this program on the part of the agents. Consequently, the professor was going to meet that need. The second year proceeded exactly the same as the first with almost identical results. At this point the chapter president contacted the professor in mid-June to find out what his plans were. When he said that he was going to reoffer this course, the chapter president asked for Institute assistance through involvement of the Board of Ethical Inquiry.

OPINION HCS-117

The Board notes with regret the lack of the professor's cooperation with the local CPCU chapter, as well as the unfortunate educational results of his efforts. However, it should also be acknowledged that the American Institute does not *require* any particular method of preparing for the national CPCU examinations. Students and instructors alike are encouraged to follow the educational advice of qualified Institute staff members, and students are offered a free program of individualized counseling. Yet, it is a well-known fact that some CPCU students do not follow sound educational advice. Some continue to rely on "cram courses" and other shortcuts which the American Institute staff members feel are of questionable educational value. But the American Institute's examination requirements do not *prohibit* participation in such courses, either as an instructor or a student. Nor would an instructor who did so violate any law. Thus, the issue in the hypothetical case is whether the professor's approach is otherwise unethical under the *Code*.

Unless a chapter member or other person was willing to file a formal complaint against the professor, the case would be dismissed as frivolous and *prima facie* without merit. Even a complaint would likewise be dismissed unless there was satisfactory evidence of a *Rule* violation. If a complaint was filed in this case, it would probably allege violations of *R6.3, R4.1,* and *R3.2.* Let us briefly consider each.

Rule 6.3 stipulates that a "CPCU shall not knowingly misrepresent or conceal any limitations on the CPCU's ability to provide the. . . quality of professional services required by the circumstances." It would be difficult for an instructor to conceal the general results of his previous CPCU classes. The Institute releases to CPCU chapters the names of the area candidates who successfully passed one or more national examinations. The local people can at least compare the list with the number of persons who initially enrolled in a particular class (and they can sometimes determine who actually sat for a particular exam). The professor could have violated the *Rule* by misrepresenting the quality of services he would provide especially if he led students to believe he would guarantee that they would pass the national examination. But there is no evidence of the latter in the description of the case.

The criteria of *G4.1* would seem to be met well enough for the Board to hear an allegation of incompetence under *R4.1*. Nonetheless, the application of the *Rule* is a bit clouded by the fact that most CPCU instructors are part-time volunteers whose primary occupational duties are owed to employers or clients. More important, evaluating the competence of an instructor is an inherently difficult task. It is done satisfactorily by some educational institutions, but it would be unfair for the Board to evaluate the ethics of CPCU instructors according to the American Institute's criteria for course effectiveness, since (1) CPCU instructors are not employed by the American Institute, (2) professional educators do not agree on all of the criteria and methods that should be used to evaluate teaching competence, and (3) there are a number of variables which effect the results of a learning opportunity, including the motivation, background, and efforts of the students themselves. Consequently, the Board cannot find, in $R4.1$, any clear-cut basis for disciplining an instructor on ethics grounds. (An instructor could of course be disciplined under $R2.1$, just like any other CPCU, but there is no evidence that this professor breached his continuing education duty.) If the local CPCU chapter employs an instructor, as is often the case, the chapter may use whatever instructor evaluation criteria and methods it chooses.

Finally, there is the question of whether the professor violated his $R3.2$ duty by "allowing the pursuit of financial gain to interfere with the exercise of sound professional judgment and skills." As spelled out in *Opinion HCS-107*, the Board will not apply $R3.2$ to sit in judgment of the level of compensation a CPCU receives in the marketplace for his or her services since it is not the absolute level of compensation which makes professional services ethically suspect. It is whether the pursuit of any size financial gain clouded the judgment of the professional, that is, seduced him to make judgments which were not in the best interests of those served. Whether the students were unjustly harmed by this professor's financially induced and unsound professional judgment is a question of fact which cannot be determined based solely on the information given. If the facts supported such a finding, the professor would be informally admonished to cease and desist. If he did not heed the warning, the Board would reprimand him and recommend his public censure.

CASE HCS-118

Bernard Forman, CPCU, Assistant Manager of a regional office of the Old Line Insurance Company, had been working with one of the Casualty Department underwriters in an attempt to help one of the company's contractor-insureds obtain a sizable government contract. In the negotiation stage on insurance costs, there was a disagreement between Bernie and the underwriter over the amount to charge for explosion, collapse, and underground property damage ("xcu") coverage under the manuscript policy. The underwriter felt the account merited a $25,000 annual premium charge, but Bernie felt $2,000 was enough. The premium level would affect the bid and thus would be a determining factor in whether or not the contractor gets the job. Bernie told the underwriter that he was making an executive decision to charge only $2,000. The project was awarded to the contractor.

Two months after this experience, the underwriter found out that Bernie was a "silent partner" in the agency which handled the contractor's account. He feels that Bernie should remove himself from all further business decisions involving the agency, and he has requested the Board of Ethical Inquiry to take action on the specific case outlined. In order to substantiate the reasonableness of his $2,000 charge, Bernie cites the fact that the job was completed without any "xcu" losses.

OPINION HCS-118

The purpose of including the Forman Case is to clarify the application of *R4.1* and *R3.1* to a specific conflict of interest situation. As an employee, Forman has an occupational duty of loyalty to his employer. He cannot discharge that duty consistently unless he is consistently honest about matters which may affect his employer. It therefore follows that Forman's failure to disclose his role as a silent partner is a violation of his *R4.1* duty under the ethics *Code*. However, *G4.1* stipulates that the Board will not hear the matter of an alleged violation of *R4.1* until all other remedies have been exhausted. Assuming the employer discovered Forman's failure to disclose his interest in the agency, the employer might well be content to dismiss Forman and/or to take other actions without bringing an ethics complaint to the Board.

Apart from the employer's decision, the underwriter or any other person could file an ethics complaint which alleged violation of *R3.2* and *R3.1*. Forman may have been motivated by the pursuit of financial gain, but it would be very difficult to prove that he violated his *R3.2* duty because the determination of an adequate premium for "xcu" coverages leaves ample room for substantial disagreements in judgment. The application of *R3.1* is another matter entirely. And the Board does feel that Forman's failure to disclose (to his employer) his agency partnership role is an "omission of a dishonest or deceitful *nature*" within the meaning of *R3.1*. Accordingly, the Board would reprimand Forman and forewarn him of the more severe penalties which might follow an additional *Rule* violation.

CASE HCS-119

Bill Executive, CPCU, is a manager of a large branch office of a national insurance company. He often entertains his neighbors and friends and charges the expenses off to his company. His expense accounts reflect that he entertained agents. When he wants to show his appreciation to his office employees for one reason or another, he advises them to take their spouses out for an evening on the town and show it on their expense accounts as entertaining agents.

John Candidate, a young underwriter studying CPCU 10, has received permission from Bill to take Mrs. Candidate out to dinner and charge it to the company. Permission was granted because John was able to get Bill a discount on a new color TV.

Because John has real reservations about the proposed method of handling personal entertainment expenses, he has written to the Board of Ethical Inquiry to determine whether this sort of conduct would be a breach of the *Code* by Bill or himself.

OPINION HCS-119

The Bill Executive-John Candidate Case has two primary educational objectives. The first is to remind readers that John Candidate's inquiry would be promptly answered by the Ethics Counsel. Candidate would be commended for observing the spirit of the *G1.2* concept which says: "When there is good reason why a person subject to the Code should be uncertain as to the ethical propriety of a specific activity or type of conduct, that person should refrain from engaging in such activity or conduct until the matter has been clarified. Any CPCU or CPCU candidate who needs assistance in interpreting the *Code* is encouraged to request an advisory opinion from the American Institute's Board of Ethical Inquiry." John Candidate would be issued an advisory opinion, and it would later be published, with names changed to conceal identities, if it was of general import.

The second objective of the case is to address the sometimes troublesome matter of expense accounts. *R3.3* makes it clear that "a CPCU will be subject to disciplinary action for the violation of any law or regulation, to the extent that such violation suggests the likelihood of professional misconduct in the future." The *Rule* most certainly includes violations of IRS regulations as well as violations of the Internal Revenue Code (and comparable state laws and regulations). But whether such a violation suggests the likelihood of professional misconduct in the future necessarily must depend upon the facts and circumstances of a particular case. Even the most reasonable persons may justifiably disagree with those who are charged with the administration and enforcement of the tax laws.

If Bill Executive and John Candidate are complying with the tax laws, and if their employer has given Bill Executive a free hand to reward employees with generous expense account allowances, the Board sees nothing unethical about the activity of either Executive or Candidate. Yet, the description of the hypothetical case strongly suggests that Executive is running afoul of *R3.1* by engaging in "any act or omission of a dishonest, deceitful, or fraudulent nature." It appears that he may also be violating the applicable tax laws and regulations. If so, and if a proper complaint were to be filed, Executive would be severely reprimanded by the Boards, and harsher penalties would be considered. The conduct of Executive is not excused by any contention, however accurate, that "thousands of people cheat on their expense accounts." And Candidate would be forewarned that any complicity on his part would be considered "participating in or condoning" a prohibited act within the meaning of *R1.2*.

There is one final point well worth mentioning. Because the Board earnestly wishes to encourage CPCUs and CPCU candidates to request advisory opinions, they are advised to use fictitious names in making such requests. Whether they wish later to report an alleged violation or file a complaint is left to their own discretion.

CASE HCS-120

J. R. "Pinky" Smith, CPCU, is an insurance agent in a small town. He starts a promotional campaign which includes a giveaway to clients and potential clients: a pen that reads: " 'Pinky' Smith, CPCU, 25 years as an insurance professional, Bigelow 9-1999." Tom Jackson, CPCU, the only other insurance agent in town, writes to the Institute complaining of Smith's promotional effort. Jackson requests the Institute to direct Smith to cease and desist. Should Smith be disciplined for violating *R8.1*?

OPINION HCS-120

Since *R8.1* incorporates by reference the *G8.1 Guidelines*, the latter have the binding effect of *Rules*. These *Guidelines* have the broad purpose of preventing the undignified and unprofessional use of the CPCU designation and the CPCU key.

Subparagraph a.3 of *Guideline G8.1* states that the designation, initials, and key may not be affixed to any object, product, or property. Smith's use of the "CPCU" letters on a pen clearly violates this *Guideline*. It should be noted that subparagraph e of this *Guideline* allows the Management Council of the American Institute to grant exceptions. Any CPCU who contemplates a use of the designation, initials, or key that he or she believes is "dignified and professional" but that has not been explicitly authorized, may contact the Management Council for approval.

Whenever the Board feels a particular use is in violation of the *Code*, it will first request the violator to cease and desist. Additional penalties will be imposed only if the violator does not comply with the initial request. (Where an unauthorized person is using the designation, the failure to cease and desist will prompt the Institute to bring a legal action.)

CASE HCS-121

A member of the Board of Ethical Inquiry, while driving to work, hears the voice of an enchantress on his car radio: "No sweat insurance—that's what you need . . . noooooo sweat . . . turn your insurance worries over to an insurance professional—let him sweat it for you . . . call Jim Counselor, CPCU, at Walnut 8-6868 . . . and that's it baby . . . no sweat." The member of the Board wonders if Mr. Counselor, a leading insurance broker and a part-time teacher of CPCU classes, has allowed his advertising agency to commercialize the CPCU designation in an undignified and unprofessional manner. Specifically, does the ad copy violate the *G8.1 Guidelines*, which have been incorporated by reference into *Rule R8.1* of the *Code of Professional Ethics*?

OPINION HCS-121

In this case, mindful of the *G8.1* criterion of dignity, the Board feels the ad copy pushes the upper limits of the boundary between good and bad taste. Although standards and values do vary, the Board would be remiss in its duty if it totally acquiesced to the imagination of an advertising agency that, in the eyes of many, compromises the dignity of the CPCU designation. The Board's action would thus be to request Mr. Counselor to cease and desist, and a copy of the *G8.1 Guidelines* would be forwarded to him with an extra copy for the advertising agency.

CASE HCS-122

"A" graduated with a degree in literature and was employed immediately after graduation by the "CBC" Insurance Agency. He received a brief, two-week training course and was encouraged to start selling all lines of personal insurance coverages. In some cases other agents accompanied "A" on his calls, but he often had to make sales presentations by himself. "A" was not successful, possibly because he felt that his knowledge of insurance coverages was inadequate.

Because of his field experience, "A" was offered a position as Director of Sales Promotion for a small life insurance company. "A" had been in his new position only a short time when the Director of Personnel died. Although "A" had no genuine experience in personnel, he assumed the top personnel position. In the past two years "A" has gained valuable on-the-job experience, but he has never attempted to increase his level of competence by taking courses, reading articles addressing personnel issues, or by participating in any activities away from the company.

Did "A" violate the *Code* in any of the three positions mentioned above?

OPINION HCS-122

If "A" is not a CPCU or a CPCU candidate, the Board has no jurisdiction. If he is, it is likely that he violated his continuing education obligation under *R2.1* since experience alone is normally not enough to maintain one's competence in a particular position in the insurance industry.

From the case description, it is not apparent as to who might file a complaint against "A." If the employer did so and alleged a violation of *R4.1*, the Board would hear the case only under the circumstances specified in *G4.1* and discussed in several of the preceding cases. Furthermore, additional information would be needed to determine whether "A" misrepresented anything in violation of *R6.3*, or misrepresented or concealed something which would violate *R3.1*. In the absence of compelling evidence concerning the latter two *Rules*, the case would be dismissed on its merits. If he violated either or both of the latter two *Rules*, disciplinary penalties would obviously be in order.

Index

M

Misrepresentations, *20, 22*

P

Penalties, under Discretionary
    Rules, *39*
Preamble of the Code, *1*
Professional competence, *7*

R

Revocation or suspension of the
    privilege to use the CPCU
    designation, *2, 39*
Rules of Professional Conduct
    allowing personal gain to inter-
        fere with sound professional
        judgment, *11*
    confidential information, treat-
        ment of, *20*
    continuing education, *8*
    cooperation with an enforcing
        tribunal, *29*
    definition of, *1*
    diligent performance of occupa-
        tional duties, *15*
    disclosure of information to
        regulatory authorities, *18*
    dishonest, deceitful, or fraudu-
        lent acts or omissions, *11*
    encouraging other insurance
        practitioners to improve their
        professional competence, *18*
    enforceability of, *2*
    improving the functioning of the
        insurance mechanism, *15*
    indirect violation of the Rules, *5*

keeping informed of legal limita-
        tions on the scope of profes-
        sional activities, *20*
    misrepresenting or concealing
        limits on a CPCU's profes-
        sional abilities, *20*
    misrepresenting the nature of the
        CPCU designation, *24*
    misrepresenting techniques,
        products, or services, *22*
    obedience to all Rules of Profes-
        sional Conduct, *5*
    personnel policies and practices,
        18
    providing objective information to
        the public, *22*
    reporting the unauthorized use of
        the CPCU designation, *28*
    supporting the CPCU candidacy
        of another person, *28*
    supporting efforts to improve the
        competence and ethics of
        insurance practitioners, *18*
    unauthorized representation of
        the American Institute, *24*
    use of the CPCU designation and
        key, *24*
    violation of laws or regulations,
        11

U

Unauthorized practice of law, *21*
Use of the CPCU designation and
    CPCU key, *24*

V

Violation of laws or regulations, *11*